TOTALLY GROSS EXPERIMENTS AND ACTIVITIES

66 Gruesome STEAM Science and Art Activities

Susan Martineau
Illustrations by Martin Ursell

FOR YOUNG READERS

T0077830

First published in the United Kingdom by b small publishing limited, East Horsley, England 2014. This paperback edition published by Racehorse for Young Readers, 2019.

Racehorse for Young Readers books may be purchased in bulk at special discounts for sales promotion, corporate gifts, fund-raising, or educational purposes. Special editions can also be created to specifications. For details, contact the Special Sales Department, Racehorse for Young Readers, 307 West 36th Street, 11th Floor, New York, NY 10018 or info@skyhorsepublishing.com.

Racehorse for Young Readers ™ is a pending trademark of Skyhorse Publishing, Inc.®, a Delaware corporation.

Visit our website at www.skyhorsepublishing.com.

10 9 8 7 6 5 4 3 2 1

Manufactured in China, 2018
This product conforms to CPSIA 2008

Library of Congress Cataloging-in-Publication Data is available on file.

Cover design by Louise Millar
Cover illustration by Martin Ursell

Print ISBN: 978-1-63158-313-1
Ebook ISBN: 978-1-63158-317-9

SLIMY SCIENCE
AND
AWESOME
EXPERIMENTS

Before You Begin

Most of these experiments give you pretty immediate and stunning results. Some of them take longer and need more patience—but they are worth it!

You don't need any special equipment to do the experiments. They use things you will probably have about the house already—like old bottles, vinegar, tinfoil, scissors, paper, and so on.

Read through the whole experiment before you begin. If it doesn't work the first time, try again! You could keep notes or even draw up your results like a real professional.

Remember never to play with heat or chemicals, and don't forget to tidy up afterwards!

Always ask a grown-up for permission before you start. Sometimes you will need a bit of help from an adult.

Sense-sational Science

Our senses of smell, sight, touch, and taste all play a vital part in telling us what things are. Is it edible? Is it fresh or stale? Is it bitter or sweet? See what happens when you can't use all of your senses to identify things.

Squish 'n Sniff

Get your friends squelching their fingers in gunk! You can choose your own grungy ideas too, but remember to make sure no one tastes the stuff. Just squish and sniff!

What you will need:
- 5 small bowls or saucers
- 5 different squishy substances,
  e.g. honey, mustard, shampoo, ketchup, toothpaste
- scarf
- tissues

1 In each bowl or saucer pour a dollop of a different substance. Make sure your friends are not looking.

2 Lightly blindfold a brave friend with the scarf. Hold their finger and stick it into one of the substances.

3 Ask your friend to sniff the stuff on their finger and tell you what they think it is. Wipe the finger and try the next bit of gunk.

Weird or What?

One of the smelliest flowers ever is also the largest in the world. The rafflesia flower measures up to 3 feet across and is found in Malaysia and Indonesia. It might look lovely, but it smells like rotting meat!

Tricky Tastebuds

This is a tricky test for your tastebuds. Try it out on your family and friends. You could think of other foods to sample too.

What you will need:
- potato
- apple
- cucumber
- peeler and knife
- plate
- paper towel
- scarf

Weird or What?

When it is slurping up bugs, a toad can flick its tongue out and back again in one tenth of a second.

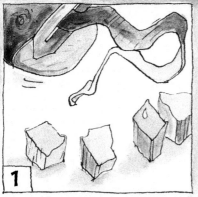

1

Peel the vegetables and fruit. Cut a few chunks of each. Make them about the same size.

paper towel

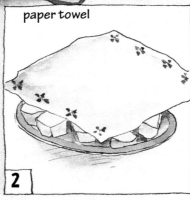

2

Put the chunks on a plate and cover them up. Do not let anyone see which is which.

3

Lightly blindfold a friend and ask them to hold their nose. Feed them a piece of each food and see if they can tell you what it is.

Fact File ▷▶

Your tastebuds are amazing! Touch the tip of your tongue with a clean, wooden popsicle stick and the wood will taste sweet. At the sides of your tongue it will taste sour. Right at the back (careful!) it will taste bitter.

Bouncing Light

Mirrors are great for magic effects. By holding them in different positions next to pictures or photos you can make things look very strange.

What you will need:

- glue
- passport photo of yourself (from a photo booth)
- small rectangular makeup mirror

1 Glue your photo on top of the face in the box below. Make sure the top of your head lines up with the horizontal line, and your nose is over the vertical one.

2 Stand one edge of the mirror on the vertical dotted line. Gradually slide it to the right—and you've conjured up a twin! Glue your photo on top of this face, in the same position.

3 Now place the mirror on the horizontal line and—wow!—you're doing acrobatics.

horizontal

vertical

Weird or What?

Modern-day mirrors are made of a sheet of glass with a very thin coat of silver on the back. Before they were invented, people used polished metal to check how bad their spots were! For some weird reflections, look at yourself in each side of a shiny spoon.

Fact File ▷▷

In this experiment you see the photo in two different ways. When you look at the picture itself, light bounces directly off the photo into your eyes. But the image you see in the mirror is light bouncing off the photo, on to the shiny surface of the glass, and *then* into your eyes.

If you have two small mirrors, stand them on their edges, facing each other, on each side of the photo. Count how many of you you can see.

Mighty Magnifier

Make a simple magnifying glass with cardboard and plastic wrap. You could use this to inspect the results of your experiments, for example the Crystal Crust on page 13.

What you will need:

- cardboard or an empty tape roll (any size)
- scissors
- plastic wrap
- clear tape
- a dead insect (optional)

1

If using cardboard, cut a strip about six inches long. Tape the ends together to make a circle.

2

Cut a piece of plastic wrap big enough to cover and overlap the edges of the circle or empty tape roll. Keep it taut and tape around the sides.

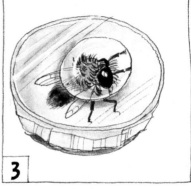

3

Place the magnifier over the insect or the drawings below, and gently plop a few drops of water onto the plastic wrap surface. Look through the water at the superbugs!

Fact File ▷▶ The glass lens of a magnifying glass is curved and changes the angle of the rays of light. This makes things look larger and more detailed. Here the water works like a lens.

Eggsperiments

Floating Eyeball

Not for the fainthearted!

What you will need:

- 1 uncooked fresh egg
- waterproof felt-tip pens
- large glass jam jar
- tablespoon
- lots of salt

The Fresh Egg Test

Place an uncooked egg in a glass bowl of water. If it lies down horizontally then it is fresh. If one end starts to rise to the surface this means the egg has more air inside it and is less than fresh. An egg that stands up is not what you want for breakfast!

1

Draw an eyeball on the egg using the felt-tip pens. Let the ink dry.

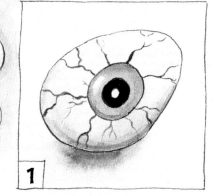

2

Fill the jam jar with very warm water. Gently lower the egg into the jar using the spoon.

3

Gradually stir one tablespoon of salt after another into the water and watch that eyeball begin to lift off the bottom. Ugh!

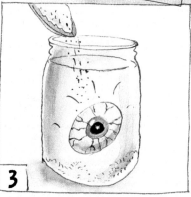

DEAD SEA

Fact File ▷▷ Just as the salt in the sea holds you up when you are swimming, the salty water supports the weight of the egg. The saltier the water the better it will float.

The Incredible Rubber Egg

How do you take the shell off a hard-boiled egg without cracking it? It's very simple and here's how.

What you will need:
- 1 hard-boiled egg, with shell on
- glass of vinegar

1 Put the egg into the vinegar. Leave it undisturbed for 3 days. You will see some wonderful scum!

2 Take the egg out of the vinegar and rinse it off. The shell will rub off.

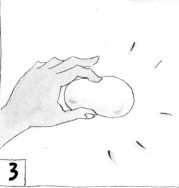

3 Give the egg a poke with your finger. Squeeze it gently. What does it feel like? It may even bounce!

Fact File ▷▶ The acid vinegar "eats up" the calcium carbonate shell, just leaving the inner membrane, or skin, of the egg behind. This makes it feel very rubbery.

Salty Stuff

The Magic Ice Cube

Amaze your friends and family with this cool trick.

What you will need:
- 1 ice cube
- glass of cold water
- 6-inch length of sewing thread
- salt
- teaspoon

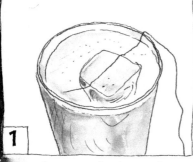

1 Gently pop the ice cube into the glass of water. Carefully place one end of the thread across the top of the floating cube.

2 Where the thread touches the ice, sprinkle salt over it with a spoon.

3 Wait for about 30 seconds and carefully lift the string. The cube will come too.

Weird or What?

If you piled up all the salt in the world's oceans and seas, it would cover all of Europe with a salt mountain 3 miles deep.

Fact File ▷▶ Because salt lowers the freezing point of water, it melts the ice a little. The thread sinks into a little pool of water, which refreezes, trapping the thread.

Crystal Crust

Salt is made of tiny grains, or crystals. You can make your own colony of salt crystals. Don't forget to ask a grown-up to help with the hot water stage of this experiment.

What you will need:
- 1 thick plastic beaker
- boiling water
- salt
- tablespoon
- piece of paper or paper towel

Weird or What?

Believe it or not, one quart of blood has the same amount of salt in it as one quart of sea water!

Take care! Hot!

1

2

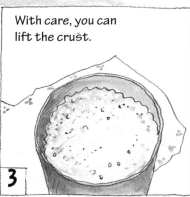

With care, you can lift the crust.

3

Ask a grown-up to help you fill the beaker with boiling water. Stir in 2–3 tablespoons of salt. Keep adding salt until no more will dissolve.

Cover the beaker with the paper or paper towel, and leave the water to cool. Wait for about 30 minutes.

Lift the paper and you will see a lovely, solid crust of salt crystals on top of the water.

You can use the magnifier on page 9 to look at the salt crystals more closely.

Fact File ▷▷
Salt crystals will dissolve more easily in warm water than in cold. As the water cools down, some of the salt that dissolved when the water was warm will turn back into crystals again.

Whizz, Bang, Burp

Ghastly Gassy Creatures

Watch these monsters expand before your eyes! You can make a whole family of them if you like. Make your designs as big as possible on the uninflated balloons. To make your own stickers, color in and cut out plain sticky labels.

What you will need:
- balloons
- bought or homemade gruesome stickers (e.g. eyeballs, fangs)
- small funnel
- teaspoon
- baking soda
- vinegar
- small, empty, clean bottles

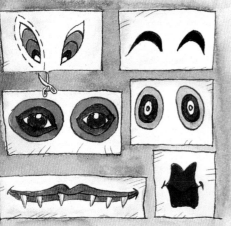

You could try some of these ghastly ideas.

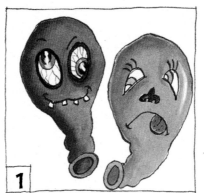

1 Position your stickers firmly on each balloon to make horrible faces or creatures.

Tap the funnel to help it go down.

2 Using the funnel, spoon 3 heaping teaspoons of baking soda into each balloon.

3 Fill each bottle a third full with vinegar and fit the neck of a balloon over each one. Don't let any baking soda fall in yet.

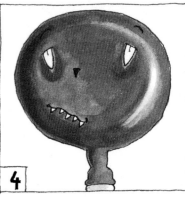

4 Now hold each balloon up and let all the baking soda fall into the vinegar.

Vinegar stings your eyes, so take care. Wash any spills with plenty of water.

Fact File ▷▷ When the baking soda falls into the vinegar it causes a chemical reaction which produces carbon dioxide gas. This then blows up the balloon for you.

Balloon Belcher

A simple and safe chemical reaction helps you create some very satisfying sound effects. The vinegary smell makes it even more realistic!

What you will need:
- 1 gassy creature from previous page

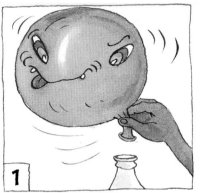

1 Carefully ease the balloon, full of gas, off the bottle. Hold the end tightly closed.

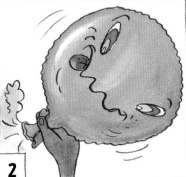

2 Slowly let some gas out to make the balloon burp. Practice will make perfect!

Weird or What?

Bacteria in your intestines usually produces about 3 pints of gas each day!

Slimy World

Create a slithery worm paradise. To find your slimy friends, look in freshly dug soil, under large stones and logs, or anywhere damp and shady. See if you can spot worm casts—swirls of earth made as soil passes through a worm's body—deposited on the surface.

What you will need:
- shoe box with lid
- clear tape
- pencil
- large empty plastic bottle
- scissors
- 3–4 large beakers of soil
- 1–2 large beakers of sand
- leaves and grass
- 3–4 fat earthworms

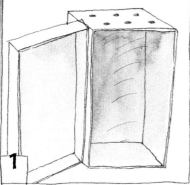

1 Tape the lid to the box to make a "door." Push the pencil into the top of the box to make air holes.

Ask an adult to help with cutting.

Don't make it too damp.

2 Cut the top off the bottle and fill it with alternating layers of soil and sand. Sprinkle with water.

Handle your worms gently.

3 Place some leaves and grass on top. Gently place your worms on them.

Fact File ▷▶ Worms are a gardener's best friend. They pull vegetation down into the soil, which makes it rich in nutrients for plants. Their tunnels let air and water into the earth, too.

Weird Worm Fact

Giant earthworms up to 10 feet long can be found in Australia, South Africa, and South America. Just think how much soil a worm that size can shift!

4 Put the bottle in the box and close the "door." Leave in a shed or cool, dark place for 4–5 days.

5 Open the "door" and you will see your worms have made tunnels through the soil and sand layers and pulled some food down with them.

Worm Health Warning

Please set your worms free after a few days!

Volcanic Eruption

Make your own volcanic special effects using the simplest of ingredients. It's best to wear old clothes while doing this experiment, and to do it outside.

What you will need:
- old newspapers
- damp sand
- baking soda
- small bottle
- funnel
- vinegar
- ketchup
- tablespoon
- small jug

Weird or What?

The greatest volcanic eruption ever recorded was on the island of Krakatoa in Indonesia in 1883. The sound of it was heard 3,000 miles away in Australia and it made a gigantic tidal wave that killed more than 36,000 people. The wave was even noticed as far away as the English Channel!

The sand should come up to the top of the bottle.

1

Half fill the bottle with the baking soda. Then stand it on the newspapers and mound up the sand around it to form a small volcano.

2

Put about half the small bottle's worth of vinegar in the jug and mix in about 2 tablespoons of ketchup.

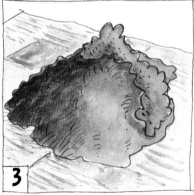

3

Using the funnel, pour the ketchup mixture into the buried bottle—and stand back!

Fact File ▷▶ The acid vinegar reacts with the alkaline baking soda to make a gas—carbon dioxide—which pushes the mixture up out of the bottle.

Underwater Fountain

Create a colorful underwater show. Use any food colorings you like. If you haven't got a large bowl or tank you can use a jug and one bottle to make a solo show.

What you will need:

- large glass jug, a tank, or large clear plastic bowl
- 2–3 small glass bottles
- 2–3 different food colorings

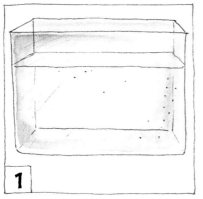

1

Pour cold water into the jug, bowl, or tank until it is three-quarters full.

2

Fill the bottles with warm water and add a different coloring to each.

3

Place the bottles in the tank so that the tops are well below the surface. Now watch the swirling show.

Upside-down Fountains

Drop ice cubes made from colored water into a jug of cold water. At first they will float, but as the ice melts colored water will swirl downwards, as the melting ice water is colder than the water around it.

Fact File ▷▶ Warm water rises and cold water sinks. This is why the warm colored water rises, and why the cold colored water drifts to the bottom.

Invisible Ink

Write up your scientific notes so that no one else can see them. You can use onion juice instead of lemon, but it might make you cry!

What you will need:
- 1 lemon
- small bowl or egg cup
- plain white paper
- fine paintbrush or an old, empty fountain pen
- oven mitts or pair of kitchen tongs

1

Squeeze the lemon juice into the bowl or egg cup. Dip in your brush or pen and write on the paper.

2 3-5 mins

Ask a grown-up to help put the paper into an oven pre-heated to 325°F. Leave for 3–5 minutes.

3

Carefully remove the paper from the oven, using oven mitts or tongs. Take care—the paper is hot!

Fact File ▷▶ The heat of the oven "burns" the lemon juice. This makes it reappear like magic.

Ectoplasmic Gunk

One minute this gunk behaves like liquid, then it's a solid—wacky stuff! Make as much of this as you like and use any food coloring you want.

What you will need:
- cornstarch
- bowl
- jug of water with food coloring added
- tablespoon

1 Put some cornstarch in the bowl and add a little colored water. Stir well.

2 Gradually add more water until the gunk is about as thick as mayonnaise.

3 Jab in your spoon, or squish it in your hands, and it will feel solid. Stir it gently, or scoop some up in your hand, and it's liquid!

Fact File ▷▶ The ectoplasm behaves like a liquid when you treat it gently, as all the particles of cornstarch can slide around each other. Pushing it or squeezing it in your hands makes all the cornstarch particles jam together and act like a solid.

Jumping Bugs

Static electricity turns these little insects into jitterbugs. You could try using bug or insect stickers on the paper instead of drawing your own.

What you will need:
- colored tissue paper
- felt-tip pens or bug stickers
- scissors
- balloon

1

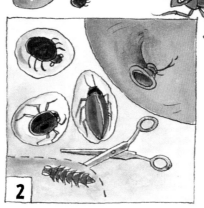

2

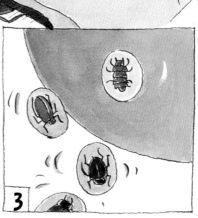

3

Draw some tiny, horrid bugs on the tissue paper or stick on your stickers. Make lots of them.

Cut them out and pile them up. Blow up the balloon and tie the end in a knot.

Rub the balloon on top of your head or on your clothes. Hold it above the bugs and watch 'em jump.

Weird or What?
The average flea can jump 200 times its own height! Just imagine how high we could jump if we were fleas!

Fact File ▷▶ Static electricity is made when some materials are rubbed together—like a balloon against your hair or a sweater. It is this kind of electricity that makes the paper jump towards the balloon.

Professor Brainstorm Cocktail

Impress your friends with this fantastic fizzer!
You probably have to be a mad scientist to drink
all of—but it is quite safe to try a little.

What you will need:
- glass of cold water, three-quarters full
- few drops of food coloring (your choice of color!)
- 1½ heaped tablespoons powdered sugar
- 3 heaped teaspoons baking soda
- 6 teaspoons lemon juice

1

Add the food coloring
to the water.

Do this where spills
won't matter.

2

Stir in the sugar and
baking soda.

3

Finally, add the lemon
juice and watch it whizz.

Fact File ▷▶ The acid lemon juice and alkaline baking soda react to make a gas—
carbon dioxide or CO_2. This is the gas that puts the fizz into fizzy drinks.

The Amazing Twister

This is very simple and very curly!

What you will need:
- clear tape
- scissors
- heavy-duty aluminum foil
- small desk lamp

Do not touch the lightbulb with fingers or foil.

1
Carefully position a length of clear tape along the edge of the foil. Trim it.

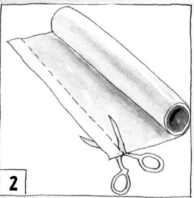

2
Cut off the strip of tape with tin foil stuck to one side.

3
Tape one end to a worktop or table and hold the lamp close to it. Just watch it start to curl and twist as the foil heats up.

Fact File ▷▶ When metal is heated it expands, but plastic does not. When metal foil and plastic tape are stuck together, the expanding foil forces the tape into curls.

Fake Fossil Footprint

Create a fascinating piece of fossil evidence. Make a cast of a footprint or a weird shape to convince your friends that something strange and prehistoric once haunted the neighborhood. You can use a muddy patch of garden instead of a box of sand.

What you will need:
- 1 cup of cold water
- 2 cups of plaster of Paris (from a hardware store)
- bowl or old plastic pot
- small cardboard box with about 7 cm of sand in it

1 Press the shape of your print into the sand or mud using your hands, feet or any other interesting-shaped object.

2 Pour the water into the bowl and sprinkle the plaster over it. Leave for 2 minutes. Then mix well with a clean hand to smooth any lumps. Leave for 4 minutes.

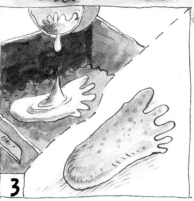

3 Pour the plaster into your shape, and clean the bowl straight away. Leave the plaster to set, then lift out your fossil evidence.

Fact File ▷▶
Fossils are the preserved remains or traces of plants and animals. Without them we would not know what prehistoric creatures looked like or when they lived. A trace fossil—like a dinosaur footprint—is the mark made by an animal while it was alive, preserved in later layers of soil and rock.

Pus-filled Boil

A gross experiment to test the nerve of your best friend.

What you will need:

- red and yellow (or green) food colorings
- some Q-tips
- vaseline
- teaspoon
- small bowl or egg cup
- a tissue

1 Choose where you want your oozing boil to be, and paint or dab a little red food coloring onto your skin.

Use a fresh Q-tip for mixing.

2 Mix a little vaseline with the yellow or green coloring in the bowl or egg cup. Put a blob on the red food coloring patch.

3 Tear a single layer of tissue to fit over the blob. Place on top and seal the "pus" inside, smoothing down the edges of "skin."

Dead SKIN

Weird or What?

Your skin never stops growing. Dead skin falls off, takes the dirt with it, and more skin cells are constantly produced. About 8.5 pounds of skin flakes off you every year. Dust is mostly made up of old bits of you!

Fact File ▷▶

Pus is putrid stuff. It is made of infection-fighting body fluids, dead cells, and dead bacteria.

26

GRUESOME GRUB AND DISGUSTING DISHES

Before You Begin

To get the best results from your gruesome cooking, here are a few tips:

Once you've chosen a recipe it's a good idea to read it all the way through and get all your equipment and ingredients ready before you start. The recipes list exactly what you will need.

You should always have a grown-up standing by to help with any recipe steps where you need to heat food or use a sharp knife.

Keep some oven mitts handy, too, for recipes involving hot food.

Always wash your hands and put on an apron before cooking, and make sure your work surfaces are nice and clean.

Afterwards . . . don't forget to wash up!

Unless otherwise mentioned, all the recipes serve 4 people.

All the spoon measurements are level ones unless the recipe says otherwise.

If you use a fan oven please reduce the temperature by at least 10–15 degrees. You may need to reduce the cooking time too.

Don't forget that all the ideas here are just to get you started. Have fun experimenting with your own creations too.

Beheaded Alien

A perfect dessert that is easy to make, and yummy to eat but looks really . . . yuk!

What you will need:

- 2 boxes of Jell-O
- 6 marshmallows
- Six half-inch lengths of dry pasta
- 2 licorice whirls or 2 candies
- measuring jug
- 5 cup heatproof bowl
- plate

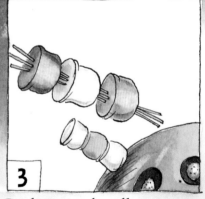

Use slightly less water to make a firmer jelly.

1

2

3

Following the instructions on the boxes, make the Jell-O. Pour it into the bowl and put it in the fridge until set firm.

Dip the bowl in a sink of hot water for a few minutes to ease the Jell-O. Carefully turn it out onto a plate.

Push 3 marshmallows onto 3 pieces of dry pasta to create a tentacle. Repeat. Push into Jell-O. Position the eyes. Serve immediately.

Puke on Toast

A quick and easy snack and very tasty. Just close your eyes while you eat it!

What you will need:

- 4 eggs
- 4 ounces milk
- salt and pepper
- 2 teaspoons butter
- 1 tomato, diced
- 1 slice of ham, cut into small pieces
- 1 cooked carrot, diced (optional)
- 4 slices of toast
- bowl and wooden spoon
- saucepan (nonstick)

1 Break the eggs into a bowl. Add the milk and beat together. Add salt and pepper to taste.

2 Melt the butter over a medium heat and add the egg mixture. Stir until the mixture begins to solidify. Keep stirring!

3 When the mixture is firm but not dry or burnt, stop heating and quickly stir in the tomato, ham, and carrot (if using).

4 Spoon onto the pieces of toast and eat immediately.

31

Disgusting Dips

A selection of squishy mixtures to dip into. You can dunk sticks of carrot, sweet red and yellow pepper, breadsticks, cucumber, and chips into the gunk.

Yuckamole

What you will need:
- 1 ripe avocado
- 2 heaping tablespoons cottage cheese
- 1–2 teaspoons lemon juice
- 1 tablespoon ketchup
- salt and pepper
- knife and fork
- bowl

1 Peel and mash the avocado using a fork. Add all the other ingredients.

2 Serve immediately in a bowl. If you leave it, it will gradually look yuckier and yuckier!

Cement

What you will need:
- 1 cup cottage cheese with pineapple
- 2–3 tablespoons cream cheese
- 6 green grapes, seeded and chopped very small
- 1.5 teaspoons soy sauce
- some slices of toast
- bowl and spoon
- knife

1 Mix all the ingredients together. Add more soy sauce, if you like, to make the cement greyer.

2 Cut the toast into shovel shapes to serve with the cement.

Nasty Nibbles

These yucky lunchtime tidbits can be made using muffins, rolls, sliced bread, or toast—whatever you prefer.

Mouse Trap

Half cut through a muffin or soft roll. Stuff with shredded lettuce and place half a hard-boiled egg inside. Mix a little mayonnaise with ketchup and dribble this over the "mouse." Add a piece of cooked spaghetti or a strip of cheese for a tail. Be careful as you bite into it!

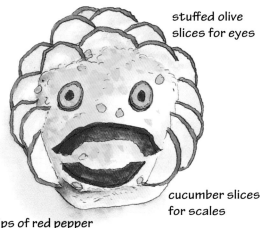

stuffed olive slices for eyes

cucumber slices for scales

strips of red pepper to make fishy lips

Fish Face

Drain a small tin of tuna and mix with a little Greek yogurt or mayonnaise. Mix in some drained, canned corn. Dollop the mixture on top of bread or toast and create your sinister fishy face.

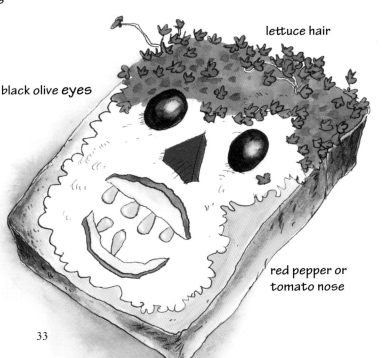

lettuce hair

black olive eyes

red pepper or tomato nose

Egg Head

Make a tasty troll face using a topping of finely chopped hard-boiled egg and cucumber mixed with mayonnaise.

cucumber lips and corn teeth

Blood and Guts

This is a really filling supper dish with a deliciously gory sauce! Use a mixture of red, green, and white spaghetti, rigatoni, or pasta knots for a great gutsy look.

Keep the lid on the saucepan.

1

Heat the oil in the medium saucepan and fry the onion and carrot until soft.

What you will need:

- ³/4–1 cup dried pasta per person
- 1 tablespoon olive or vegetable oil
- 1 medium onion, chopped
- 1 carrot, chopped very small or grated
- 14 ounce can of chopped tomatoes
- pinch of mixed herbs
- salt and pepper
- 1 large and 1 medium saucepan (with lid)
- wooden spoon
- colander

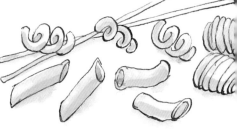

2

Add the tomatoes, herbs, salt, and pepper. Stir and let it simmer gently, uncovered, for about 20 minutes.

Cook until the pasta is soft but still has some "bite."

3

Fill the large pot three quarters full with water. Add ¹/2 teaspoon salt, bring it to a boil, and add the pasta. Cook for 10–12 minutes.

4

Strain the pasta. Toss it in the sauce before serving. (This makes it look gutsier!)

Throat Throttler

A sinister drink that Dracula would be proud of. It's even got fangs to match. Try drinking while wearing them!

For each person you will need:

- 1 thick slice of cucumber
- 1 glass soda
- 1 dessert spoon ice cream (any flavor)
- knife
- tall glass
- 2 straws

1

First cut out your fangs from the cucumber slice as shown. You could try them on too!

2

Half fill the glass with soda. Add the ice cream and then top up with more soda as it froths. Pop in the straws, decorate with the fangs, and serve.

For an extra fright you could drop in a lychee or two before adding the ice-cream. Use canned or fresh, peeled ones. Just watch your friends' faces when they see what's lurking in their glasses.

Creepy Cakes

These are brilliant for Halloween parties or any time you want to make your friends shudder. Use the basic cake mixture recipe for all three variations.

Eyeball Cakes

What you will need to make 16–18 cakes:

- 1 stick softened butter or margarine
- 1/2 cup caster sugar
- 2 eggs
- 1/2 cup self-raising flour
- 1/2 cup powdered sugar, sifted
- small packet of chocolate chips
- red food coloring
- bowl
- wooden and metal spoons
- 18 cupcake wrappers
- muffin pan
- cooling rack
- round-ended knife
- small paintbrush (clean!)

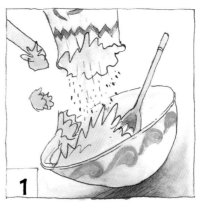

1 Cream the butter, or margarine, and sugar together until they are pale and fluffy.

2 Beat in the eggs, one at a time, with a tablespoon of flour with each. Fold in the rest of the flour with a metal spoon.

3 Cool on the rack.

Put cupcake wrappers in muffin pan. Spoon in equal amounts of mixture. Bake in the oven at 375°F for 15–20 minutes until risen and golden.

Mix the powdered sugar with 1 tablespoon hot water until smooth and not too runny.

4 When cool, use the knife to cover the top of cakes with icing. Put a chocolate chip in the center of each. Using the brush, draw veins on the icing with red food coloring.

Bat Bites

Make chocolate cupcakes by using 1 tablespoon cocoa powder instead of 1 tablespoon flour.

Cut off top of cakes and halve the tops to make wings.

You will need some chocolate spread or chocolate icing. Spoon a small blob on to the center, position the wings, and finish with silver balls for eyes.

Spider Sponges

Ice the cakes before decorating. You will need candies of different sizes and colors.

black candy for body

small candies for eyes

licorice lace legs

Snail Buns

You will need licorice whirls with or without colored centers.

Press licorice whirl down on top of a thick layer of white icing. Don't worry if your snails don't hold their heads up very high!

Cut a slit down a whirl to make snail antlers.

Munch a Monster

A snack to give your family and friends a real scare.
Instead of making your own pizza crusts you could buy ready-made,
individual-sized ones from the supermarket.

What you will need to make 4 small monsters:

- ²/₃ cup plain flour
- 2 teaspoons easy-blend yeast
- 1 teaspoon salt
- ¹/₂ cup warm water
- 14 ounce can of chopped tomatoes, drained
- 1 tablespoon tomato purée
- salt and pepper
- pinch of mixed herbs (optional)
- 1 large and 1 small bowl
- wooden spoon
- plastic bag, dusted inside with flour
- rolling pin
- well-greased baking tray

1

Mix the flour, yeast, and salt in the large bowl. Add the water and mix to form a soft dough.

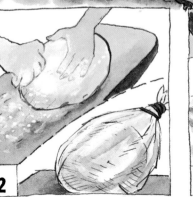

2

Knead the dough with floured hands for a few minutes. Put it in the bag and leave in a warm place for 15–20 minutes.

Dust work surface with flour.

3

Mix the tomatoes with the tomato purée, salt and pepper, and herbs, if using. Divide the dough into 4 balls. Roll or press each one out into a circle about 6 inches across.

4

Place the circles on the baking tray and spread tomato sauce on each one. Add your toppings before baking at 400°F for 20–25 minutes.

Let your imagination run away with you to create some really monstrous toppings. Corn kernels make scary teeth. Layers of sliced zucchini, pepperoni, and stuffed olives make ghastly eyes. Use a slice of mushroom for a nose and make hideous hair out of yellow, red, and green pepper.

Try cutting the dough circle into other awful shapes—like a skull!

Snot Surfers

A tasty bowl of slime soup topped with brave surfers.
Eat them quickly before they fall into the gunky depths!

What you will need:

- 1 medium onion
- 3 medium leeks, thoroughly washed
- 1 large potato, peeled
- two tablespoons of butter
- 4 cups chicken or vegetable stock
- salt and pepper
- 4 slices of toast
- knife
- large saucepan with lid
- wooden spoon
- sieve (or blender) and bowl
- gingerbread man cutter

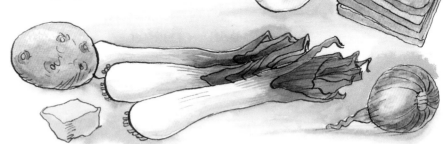

1

Stir occasionally.

Thinly slice the onion, leeks, and potato. Cook gently in the butter for 10 minutes. Keep the lid on.

2

Add the stock and salt and pepper. Simmer for about 15 minutes. Then sieve or liquidize in a blender.

3

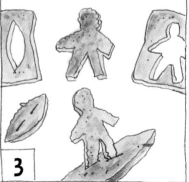

Cut out your toast surfers and their surfboards. Make slits in the boards and insert the surfers' feet. Serve one on each bowl of soup.

Slushy Slurps

Use as many different flavored juices and concentrates as you like to make these poisonous-looking, but definitely delicious, drinks.

What you will need:
- fruit juices and diluted juice concentrates of your choice
- ice cube trays
- strong plastic bags and ties
- rolling pin
- glasses and straws

grape

pineapple

lime

orange   lemon   apple

1 Pour the juices and concentrates into ice cube trays. Put them in a freezer overnight or for a few hours.

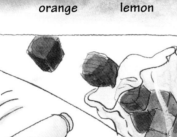

2 Pop the ice cubes out, one color at a time, into a plastic bag. Seal the bag and bash the cubes with the rolling pin to crush well.

3 Layer the colors as garishly as you like in glasses. Slurp through a straw.

Dead Man's Hand

A gruesome centerpiece for any party table, this will really revolt your friends and family. You need to put it in the fridge to defrost slightly before serving—just until the fingers wiggle!

What you will need:

- 1 large new rubber glove, very well washed
- 1 box of yellow or orange Jell-O
- 1 box of red Jell-O
- red food coloring
- red licorice laces
- measuring cup
- jug and spoon
- 3 clothespins
- large plate
- scissors
- small paintbrush (clean!)

Make sure the Jell-O is well dissolved in the hot water.

1 Break the Jell-O into pieces. Place in the jug and dissolve in 10 ounces boiling water. Then add 10 ounces cold water.

You really need two people for this.

2 Over a sink, pour mixture into the glove and seal it well by folding over the opening at least twice and pinning it firmly.

3 Place the hand palm side down on a plate. Space out the fingers. Put it in a freezer overnight.

4 Cut the glove, bit by bit, and gradually peel it off.

Decorating the hand:

Brush on red food coloring to make the hand look as gory as possible. Don't forget the stump as well as the nails!

As the hand defrosts the coloring will run a bit and this will make it look even creepier.

Place red licorice laces on the back of the hand for veins.

If you eat one finger first, you can really freak out your friends!

Yeti Foot

A gory, giant foot that makes you glad the rest of the creature isn't around!
Serve it with some salad or other vegetables for a complete monster meal.

What you will need:

- 4–5 medium potatoes, peeled, cut into chunks
- 2 tablespoons of butter
- 1/4 cup plain flour
- 1 egg, beaten
- 2/3 cup cheddar cheese, grated

- salt and pepper
- chunky chutney or ketchup
- large saucepan
- potato masher
- wooden spoon
- greased baking tray

1

Boil the potatoes in a pan of water until soft (about 15–20 minutes). Drain them and stir in the butter. Mash until smooth.

Sculpt and squish into shape.

2

Mix in the flour, egg, and cheese. Season to taste. Place large blobs of the mixture on the baking tray in the shape of a foot with three toes.

3

Bake in the oven at 425°F for 15 minutes until golden brown. Serve with the ketchup or chutney dribbled over it.

Bony Biscuits

These skull-and-bones biscuits are great fun to make. You could use red licorice laces to tie some bones together. Don't worry if your shapes look a bit rough around the edges—they may have been buried for some time!

What you will need to make 18-20 biscuits:

- 1 cup plain flour
- 1/2 cup caster sugar
- 1/3 cup butter or margarine
- grated rind of lemon (optional)
- 1 small egg, beaten
- a few raisins
- bowl and wooden spoon
- rolling pin
- knife
- greased baking tray
- cooling rack

1 Use only your fingertips and thumbs.

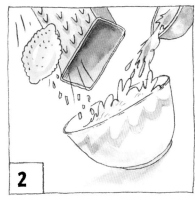

2

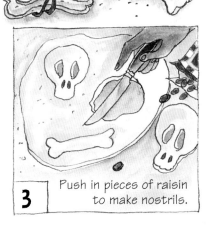

3 Push in pieces of raisin to make nostrils.

Mix the flour and sugar in the bowl. Rub in the butter or margarine until the mixture has the texture of fine breadcrumbs.

Add the lemon rind, if using, and enough egg to mix to a stiff dough.

Roll out on a floured surface and cut out your skulls and bones. Place on baking trays and bake in the oven at 350°F for 10–15 minutes. Cool on a rack.

Maggot Cocktail

Invite your friends to try this squirmy starter—it really is delicious. It looks its wriggliest in glass dishes.

What you will need:

- 1/2 lb cooked, peeled shrimp (defrosted if frozen)
- 4 tablespoons mayonnaise
- 2 teaspoons ketchup
- 2 teaspoons lemon juice
- pepper
- shredded lettuce leaves
- lemon slices
- spoon
- bowl
- 4 dishes
- greased baking tray

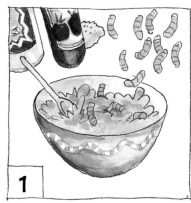

1

Mix together the mayonnaise, ketchup, and lemon juice. Add pepper to taste. Leave aside about 16 shrimp and stir the rest into the mixture.

You don't need to be too tidy!

2

Make a bed of lettuce in each dish and spoon some shrimp mixture on top.

Serve with brown bread.

3

Garnish with the lemon slices and remaining prawns. Make them look like escaping maggots! Keep in the fridge until ready to serve.

Whiffy Puffs

These look wonderful as they puff up and when you bite into them . . . phew! What a stench!

What you will need to make 8 puffs:

- 1 pound package ready-made puff pastry (defrosted if frozen)
- 40 g blue Stilton cheese
- 1 egg, beaten
- flour for dusting
- rolling pin
- 3 inch round cutter
- pastry brush
- baking tray
- knife

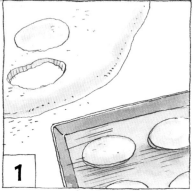

1 On a floured surface, roll out the pastry until it is 1/4 inch thick. Cut out 16 rounds. Place 8 on the baking tray.

2 Put a knob of Stilton cheese in the middle of each. Brush the pastry edges with egg. Place the remaining rounds on top. Press down and pinch the edges firmly.

3 Cut a small slit in each top. Brush on some more egg and bake in the oven at 425°F for 10–15 minutes. Serve hot.

Cow Pie Pudding

This looks disgustingly like the real thing but is a really yummy treat. If you want to add texture to your cow pie you can always mix in some dried fruits like raisins or candied cherries with the biscuit crumbs. Yum! Yum!

What you will need:

- 1/2 pound of plain graham crackers
- 8 tablespoons butter, cut into pieces
- 1 cup plain chocolate, broken into pieces
- sour apple licorice
- a few raisins

- large plastic bag and tie
- rolling pin
- mixing bowl
- 9 inch round cake tin
- cooking foil
- small saucepan
- wooden spoon

1

Put the graham crackers in the bag. Seal, and crush into tiny crumbs with the rolling pin. Empty into the bowl.

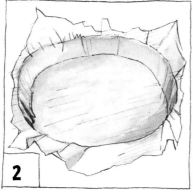

2

Line the tin with foil, making sure it goes right into the edges.

Make sure all crumbs are coated.

3

Put the butter and chocolate in the saucepan and heat gently. Stir until the chocolate is melted. Pour into the cracker mix.

4

Spoon the mixture into the tin. Press it down and use the back of the spoon to make circular patterns on top. Put the cake in fridge to set for at least 2 hours.

To decorate your cow pie:

On a large plate, arrange clumps of sour apple licorice. Lift the cow pie out of its tin and remove the foil.

Instead of licorice laces, you could use a green plate or dish as "grass."

Place it on the "grass" and decorate with a few raisin "flies" or "dung beetles."

49

Axeman's Snacks

Ideal party food for a ghoulish occasion—these are simple to make but look really horrible. Don't leave them where someone faint-hearted might find them.

What you will need:
- pack of 4 hot dogs
- 8 small soft rolls
- 1 radish
- ketchup
- wooden spoon
- knife

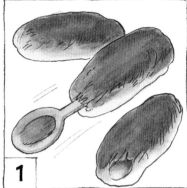

1

Use the handle of the spoon to push a hole almost all the way through each roll.

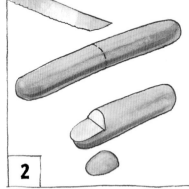

2

Spoon a little ketchup into each hole. Cut each frankfurter in half and then cut a "bed" for each nail in each closed end.

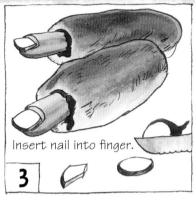

Insert nail into finger.

3

Push half a frankfurter into each roll. Cut a thin slice of radish and then a wedge from this. Trim to make a nail.

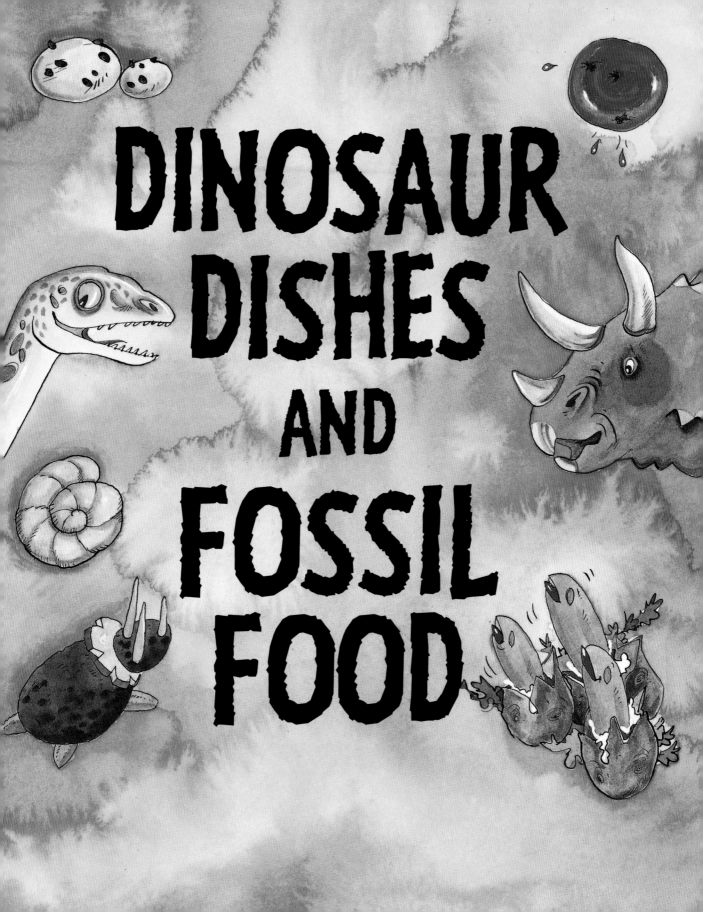

DINOSAUR DISHES AND FOSSIL FOOD

Before You Begin

You'll really impress your friends with these prehistoric dishes. They're great for dinosaur parties and fun for lunch boxes too.

When you've chosen a recipe, read it all the way through and get all of the ingredients and equipment ready before starting to cook. Wash your hands first and remember to clean up afterwards! All the recipes will serve four children unless it says otherwise.

It's a good idea to have an adult standing by when you are using the oven or cutting with sharp knives.

Always keep some oven mitts handy, too, for handling hot pans and tins.

Don't forget that these recipes are just to get you started — you can make up all sorts of fossil food yourself.

Dino Hatchlings

These poor little dinos may never make it.
A large, carnivorous beast is going to eat them—you!

What you will need:

- 4 large potatoes, scrubbed clean
- 2 hot dogs, cut in half
- ketchup
- mayonnaise or salad cream
- small pieces of red and green pepper

Prick the potatoes with a fork.

1

Bake the potatoes in the oven at 400°F for 1–1½ hours. When they are cooked they will feel soft when squeezed.

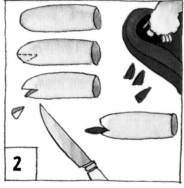

2

Cut a wedge out of each rounded hot dog end to make a mouth. Cut small triangles of red pepper and push inside for a tongue.

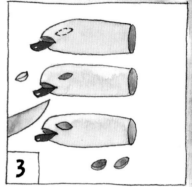

3

Cut tiny slits on each side of the mouths. Cut out slivers of green pepper and push into the slits for eyes.

Cut a cross in each potato.

4

Open the potatoes up slightly. Place a dollop of mayonnaise and some ketchup inside.

5

Push a frankfurter into each potato so that it is standing up. Nestle on a bed of salad leaves.

Egg Stealers

Oviraptors were egg thieves. That's what their name means. They were very small dinosaurs, but they could run fast and had great big front claws for grabbing eggs. Then they used their bony beaks to break them open.

55

Plesiosaur's Pond

This is a warm, swampy soup complete with prehistoric foliage. The Fossil Fodder on page 62 is pretty tasty with this.

What you will need for 4 small servings or 2 large ones:

- 1 tablespoon vegetable or olive oil
- 1 medium-sized onion, chopped small
- 2 leeks, washed and chopped
- 1 ounce red lentils
- 1/2 cup split green peas
- 4 1/4 cups vegetable stock
- pinch of dried thyme
- salt and pepper
- fresh parsley sprigs
- celery stalks with leaves on

1

Heat the oil in a large saucepan. Add the onion and leeks. Cook gently until they are soft.

2

Add the lentils, peas, stock, and thyme. Simmer for 1 hour with the lid half on until the peas are soft.

3

Add salt and pepper to taste. Roughly blend the mixture in a blender or food processor.

4

Serve the soup in bowls. Stand parsley and celery stalks around the edges.

Monster in the Lake

Plesiosaurs were long-necked reptiles that fed on fish and other reptiles. Some people think that the legendary Loch Ness Monster in Scotland is a plesiosaur that was trapped in the loch when the level of the seas went down millions of years ago. Maybe there's more than one!

Pterosaur Wings

These make a delicious snack or great party nibble for a bunch of meat-eaters.

What you will need:

- 8 chicken wings
- 3 tablespoons maple syrup
- grated zest of half an orange
- 1 tablespoon soy sauce

1

2

Turn them in the sauce once or twice.

3

Mix together the syrup, zest, and soy sauce in a small bowl.

Place the wings on a roasting tray. Pour the sauce over them.

Put them in the oven at 375°F for about 25 minutes until nicely browned.

Flying Dinos

Pterosaurs were beautiful, great flying reptiles.
Although they could fly, they were not related to birds.
Some of them were really enormous.
Quetzalcoatlus (bet you can't say that!) had a wingspan
of about 40 feet. That's bigger than a hang glider.

T. rex Ribs

Get your teeth into these juicy bones. They are a carnivore's feast and perfect for parties and lunch boxes.

What you will need:

- 1 lb pork spare ribs
- splash of vegetable or olive oil
- 1 small onion, finely chopped
- 1 garlic clove, peeled and finely chopped
- 1 tablespoon soy sauce
- 1 tablespoon clear honey
- 1½ tablespoons tomato purée
- 1 teaspoon Worcestershire sauce

1

Heat the oil in a small saucepan and fry the onion and garlic gently until softened.

2

Remove from the heat. Add all the other ingredients except the ribs. Mix thoroughly.

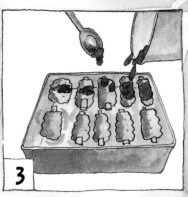

3

Put the ribs in a roasting pan and smother with the sauce mix.

4

Roast the ribs in the oven at 400°F for 1–1¼ hours. Turn them around in the sauce from time to time.

King of the Dinos

There's no doubt that Tyrannosaurus rex was a real terror!
He had huge jaws strong enough to crush bones and a mouth
big enough to swallow you whole. His teeth were as long as the
knife you use to eat your dinner.

T. rex's eyes faced forwards so that he was very good at spotting
prey. He was about 50 feet long and as tall as a two-story
house. You'd definitely have heard him coming!

Dino Dung

Make some delicious droppings for all your friends to enjoy!

What you will need to make about 10 lumps:

- 1 ½ cups self-raising flour
- pinch of salt
- 5 tablespoons butter or margarine
- 1 cup plain chocolate

- ⅓ cup caster sugar
- 1 egg, beaten
- 2 tablespoons milk

Use only your fingertips and thumbs.

1

Sieve the flour and salt into a large bowl. Add the butter or margarine and rub it into the flour.

The mixture will be quite thick.

2

Cut the chocolate into small chunks. Mix it into the flour with the sugar. Add the egg and milk.

Bake until light brown.

3

Plonk piles of the mixture on to a greased baking sheet. Bake in the oven at 350°F for about 15 minutes.

4

Place the dung on a cooling rack.

Ask a grown-up to help you take the tray out of the oven. You could serve the droppings on a bed of green licorice "grasses."

Excremental Evidence

Fossilized dinosaur droppings have a proper scientific name—coprolites. It's not surprising that most of them were pretty big! Amazingly, scientists can get an idea of what dinosaurs ate from examining this petrified poo.

Flies in Amber

Preserve some flies in your own version of prehistoric amber. You need to use very small containers—eggcups are ideal—to make these. (Remember with half a pack of Jell-O you only need half the amount of water it says on the pack.)

What you will need to make about 8:
- ½ pack orange Jell-O
- handful of raisins
- jug and spoon

1

Make the Jell-O in a jug following the instructions on the packet.

2

Allow it to cool down completely. Snip some raisins with scissors to make them "fray" a bit.

3

Pour some Jell-O mixture into 8 eggcups or small bowls. Pop 1 or 2 raisins into each. Put them in the fridge to set.

4

Dip each eggcup or bowl into warm water to loosen the Jell-O and turn them out onto plates.

Trapped in Time

Amber is the fossilized sap of trees. Many types of insect are found preserved in amber. They would have been trapped in the sap while it was still runny, millions of years ago. Some of the insects are so well preserved that you can clearly see the lacework of their wings and their color patterns. Amazing!

Fossil Fodder

Challenge your friends to fit these bones together to make part of a dino skeleton. They are delicious eaten with the Plesiosaur's Pond on page 56. Try making up your own remains—a jawbone, maybe, or some fossil feet and claws.

What you will need:

- 1 cup plain flour plus extra for dusting
- 1/2 cup finely grated cheddar cheese
- pinch of paprika or cayenne pepper

- salt and pepper
- 4 tablespoons butter or margarine
- 1 egg yolk

 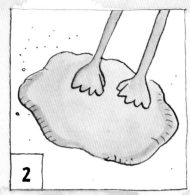 

1 Mix the flour with the cheese, salt, and both peppers. Rub in the butter or margarine, using your thumbs and fingertips.

2 Mix in the egg yolk and form the mixture into a ball of dough. Knead it a little bit.

3 Dust your worktop with flour. Roll the dough out until it is about 1/2 cm thick.

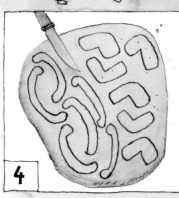

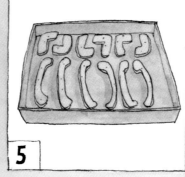

4

Cut out backbones and rib shapes as shown. Use a knife to carve them out.

5

Make as many as you like and place them on an UNGREASED baking tray. Bake in the oven at 350°F for 15 minutes.

6

Cool on a rack and then piece the backbones and ribs together.

Ammonite Whirls

Use up the off-cuts of dough to make these fossils. Roll the dough into sausages. Curl them up. Flatten slightly and score with a knife and bake for 20 minutes as above.

Dinosaur Detectives

Fossilized bones are the main evidence we have that dinosaurs even existed. Scientists have to use clever ways to work out what the dinosaurs would have looked like when they were alive. The bones have rough marks on them and these show scientists where the muscles were attached and where blood vessels may have been.

Fossil impressions of dinosaur skin have also been found and this helps fossil hunters to know if a dinosaur was covered in scales or knobbly skin. Gradually the evidence is pieced together, like a prehistoric detective story.

Ice Age Bowl

This is a fantastic centerpiece for any dinosaur party. You can serve all kinds of things in it—Glacial Deposits (see page 65) or Flies in Amber (page 61). Just don't eat the bowl! There are some great fossil-like pasta shapes in the shops. Use bowls with a gap between them of about 1 inch when the little one is inside the medium one.

What you will need:
- 4–5 handfuls of uncooked dried pasta shapes
- 1 medium freezer-safe bowl
- 1 small freezer-safe bowl
- about 16 ice cubes
- plastic bag and rolling pin
- clear tape

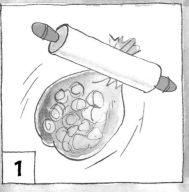

1

Put the ice cubes in a plastic bag and bash lightly with a rolling pin until they are crushed.

2 Fill the gap with more water.

Put the crushed ice into the medium bowl. Add some cold water and float the smaller bowl inside it.

3

Slide handfuls of pasta into the gap between the bowls. Spread them out evenly on the sides and underneath.

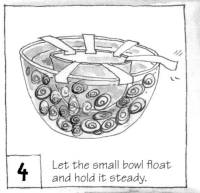

4 Let the small bowl float and hold it steady.

Put some pieces of tape across the bowls to keep the rims level with each other. Put the bowls in the freezer for the night.

5

Take off the tape. Put some warm water into the small bowl and lift it out. Dip the medium bowl into hot water and the ice bowl will slip out.

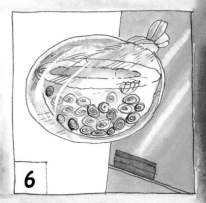

6

Pop the ice bowl into a large plastic bag and keep it in the freezer until it is needed. It can be used over and over again as long as it is put back in the freezer.

Glacial Deposits

These crunchy, icy remains look great served up in the Ice Age Bowl. Just break up some chocolate cookies and sugar wafers in a bowl. Add some spoonfuls of soft-scoop vanilla ice-cream and mix.

The Big Freeze?

How did the dinosaurs die out? Some scientists think that a massive meteorite may have crashed into our planet and caused such a large explosion that the dust and debris cut out all the sunlight. This meant that plants could not grow and so the plant-eating dinosaurs died out. The meat-eaters would have had no chance of survival either without their usual prey.

Primordial Sludge

A slime from the mists of time. This tastes a lot better than any algae would!
You could serve it in the Ice Age Bowl on page 64.

What you will need:

- 7 1/2 cups cooking apples, peeled and cored
- 1 cup caster sugar
- 1 1/4 cups water
- 1 box lime Jell-O, broken into pieces

Stir to dissolve the sugar.

1

Slice the apples. Put the sugar and water into a large saucepan and heat it gently.

Stir well to dissolve the Jell-O.

2

Add the sliced apples. Cover the pan and simmer until they are soft. Turn the heat down. Add the Jell-O. Mash the apples and Jell-O together.

3

Pour into a bowl and let the mixture cool. Chill until ready to serve.

Ancient Algae

In Shark Bay in Western Australia, living "rocks," called Stromatolites, can be found by the sea. They consist of layers of single cells of algae which are living examples of the oldest forms of life on earth. The fossilized Stromatolites that have been found in rocks in other places are thought to be more than 3.5 billion years old.

Trilobite Bites

These yummy, chunky bites are full of fossils.

To make about 12 bites:

- 7 tablespoons butter or margarine
- 2 tablespoons golden syrup
- 1 cup soft brown sugar
- 2 cups porridge oats
- pinch of salt
- ½ teaspoon ground cinnamon
- ⅓ cup whole pecan nuts

NUT ALLERGY WARNING!

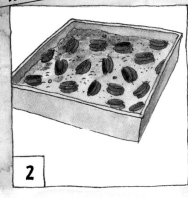

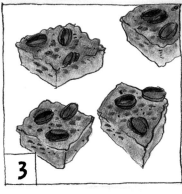

1 Melt the butter or margarine with the syrup and sugar in a pan. Remove from the heat and stir in the oats, salt, and cinnamon.

2 Tip into a 6 inch square tin and spread out evenly. Push pecans all over the surface of the mixture.

3 Bake at 325°F for 20–25 minutes. Leave to cool in the tin. Cut into chunks.

Mud Grovellers

Trilobites are the fossil relations of crabs and crayfish. Their name means "three-lobed" and you can clearly see the three parts of them in their fossils. Their eyes had many small lenses—just like a fly's. From the fossilized trails they have left in the mud, scientists have been able to tell that they lived and hunted for food on the seabed.

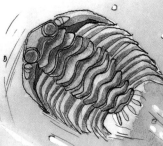

Dead Dinos

These poor Triceratops are dead delicious. You can use the basic burger mix to create other types of horned or spiky dinosaurs too. Try out different garnishes and see what you can come up with.

What you will need for the armor:
- 4 thin slices of cucumber
- 4 small "cocktail" pickles
- mixed salad leaves
- 12 pretzel or Bombay mix sticks
- ketchup

What you will need to make 4 bodies:
- 1 lb lean ground beef
- 1 small onion, very finely chopped
- 1 teaspoon mustard
- 1 teaspoon dried mixed herbs
- salt and pepper

First make your bodies:

1 Mix all the body ingredients really well in a bowl. Shape the mixture into 4 body-shaped and head-shaped blobs as shown.

2 Put them on a hot grill for 8–10 minutes. Turn once.

Prepare the dinos' armor:

1 Cut a "frill" out of each cucumber slice.

2 Cut each pickle into four.

3 Put some salad leaves on each plate.

When the bodies are cooked, put 4 pickle legs underneath each one, and place them on the leaves.

Push 3 pretzel or Bombay mix sticks into each head as shown. Make a cut in each neck and insert the cucumber "frills." Dribble ketchup down one side of each Triceratops and dig in!

Fancy Frills and Shoulder Spikes

Use carrots for Stegosaurus plates!

By the end of the time of the dinosaurs, some plant-eaters had developed amazing armor against the fierce attacks of the meat-eaters. Triceratops not only had a huge neck frill but also three horns to fend off predators. Sauropelta had bony studs all over its back and spikes sticking out of its sides. Stegosaurus had a double row of pointed plates on its back.

Fossil-hunter's Lunch

These are ideal recipes for a paleontologist. You could always add some Gastroliths from page 74 just in case you get indigestion.

Jurassic Juice

A refreshing drink for all fossil hunters. You could try out other combinations of fruits too.

For each person you will need:
- a ripe kiwi fruit
- half a large banana or a whole small one
- ½ glass of apple juice
- a stick of celery with leaves on

1 Peel the kiwi fruit and banana and chop them into chunks. Put them into a food processor or blender.

2 Measure half a glass of apple juice and add to the fruit. Blend everything together for a few seconds.

3 Pour into a tall glass and garnish with the leafy stick of celery.

Sedimentary Sandwiches

Build up layers of rock and sediment using all kinds of breads and fillings. About 4 slices of different types of bread and 3 fillings looks very geological!

Try using dark German rye bread, whole wheat, and bakery slices. See what interesting breads you can find.

Choose from the following fillings or make up your own:

- Slices of cheese
- Cream cheese mixed with chopped grapes
- Chunk tuna with mayonnaise and chopped cucumber
- Slices of ham, salami, or other cold meats
- Hummus or other spreads and dips that you like

1 Cut the crusts off the slices of bread.

2 Layer the fillings and bread slices until you have built up several layers of sediment.

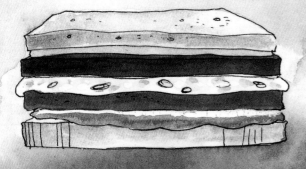

3 Slice in half and serve.

Fossil Formation

When a dinosaur died its body might sink into a river. The flesh would rot or be eaten by other creatures. The bones would gradually be covered in layers of sand and mud. Over time these sediments would turn into rock and the bones would become as hard as rock too, preserving the skeleton.

Over millions of years the layers of rock are worn away or eroded. Then the dinosaur bones are uncovered and a lucky scientist might discover them!

Mammoth Tusks in Mud

Excavate your own hairy mammoth remains from your freezer. This is some of the tastiest mud you will ever find!

What you will need for the tusks:

- 4 ripe bananas
- 4 wooden skewers, with the points snipped off
- aluminum foil

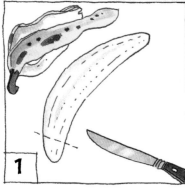 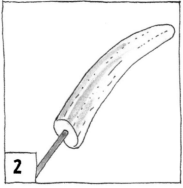 

1	**2**	**3**
Peel the bananas. Cut a little bit off the end of each one. (Eat this!)	Push a wooden skewer into the cut end of each banana. Push it as far as you can without it coming through the curved side.	Cut 4 pieces of foil and wrap each banana in one. Put in the freezer overnight.

What you will need for the mud:

- 1/2 cup dark chocolate
- 5 ounces heavy cream

1 Break up the chocolate into pieces and place in a small saucepan. Melt it gently, stirring all the time.

2 Add the cream. Whisk it into the chocolate as you heat it gently.

BE CAREFUL AS THE MUD IS VERY HOT!

To serve:

Pour the mud into individual bowls. Take the tusks out of the freezer and unwrap. Give everyone a tusk each and get stuck in the mud!

Woolly Mammoths

These enormous, hairy, elephant-like creatures lived in the cold regions of Europe, Asia, and North America during the last Ice Age. They had giant tusks—the longest fossil tusk found is about 13 feet long—but they were plant-eaters, not meat-eaters.

Deep-frozen fossils of woolly mammoths have been found in areas of the world, like Siberia, where the temperature hasn't risen above freezing for hundreds of thousands of years.

Gastroliths

Some plant-eating dinosaurs used to swallow stones and pebbles—known as gastroliths—to help them break up and digest their food. Scientists have found these stones inside the fossilized rib cages of many dinosaur skeletons. Now you can make some!

What you will need to make 15–20 gastroliths:

- 1 can of chickpeas, drained and rinsed
- 1 clove of garlic, peeled and roughly chopped
- 1½ tablespoons tahini (sesame seed paste)
- 1 egg, beaten
- ½ teaspoon ground cumin
- ½ cup breadcrumbs, preferably fresh
- salt and pepper
- pinch of cayenne pepper (optional)

1

Put the chickpeas, garlic, tahini, egg, and cumin in a food processor and blend them well.

2

Pour the mixture into a bowl and mix in the breadcrumbs, some salt and pepper, and the cayenne if you like.

3

Form the mixture into small stone shapes and place on a greased baking tray. Bake in the oven at 350°F for 15–20 minutes.

Gastrotip

Serve these stones with a squeeze of lemon juice inside some warm pita bread with salad.

Dino Digestion

Sauropods were plant-eating dinosaurs that could not really chew very well because their jaws didn't move the right way to grind up their food. Some of them, like Diplodocus, had no back teeth at all. They used to swallow branches and leaves whole and that's why they needed the help of stones in their stomachs to digest the stuff. Ow!

ASTONISHING ART AND RECYCLED RUBBISH

Before You Begin

Start a trash collection! All kinds of old junk can be transformed into amazing artwork.

boxes of all shapes and sizes

old sponges (clean!)

Make sure the trash is clean and dry before you store it. Boxes can be folded flat so they take up less room when stored.

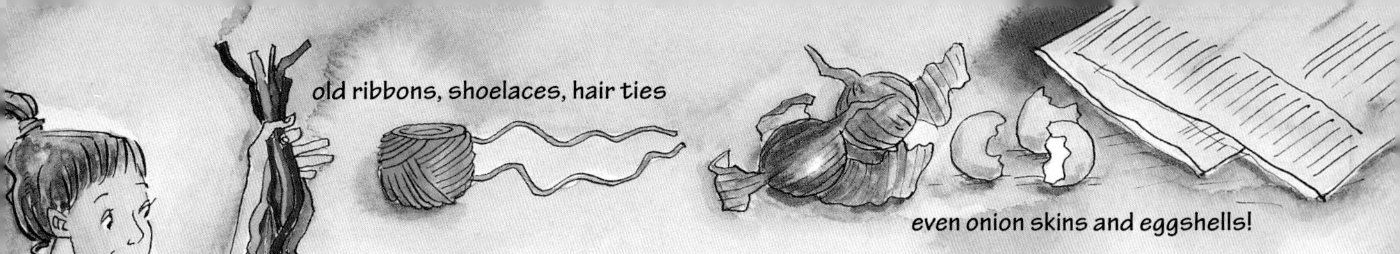

old ribbons, shoelaces, hair ties

even onion skins and eggshells!

Don't forget to use old newspapers to cover work surfaces before you begin a project. To protect your clothes you could wear an old shirt inside out! Old detergent bottle caps make great containers for paints and glue. Empty chip tubes are good for storing pencils and felt-tips.

old clothes

can tabs

Don't get too carried away collecting trash— stop when you have a boxful and get rolling on some of the ideas in this book!

tinfoil galore

cardboard, colored paper, glitzy wrapping paper

detergent bottle caps

old photos and postcards

corks

You will need a bit of grown-up help in one or two places. These have been marked with this special symbol.

!

The Original Fanny Pack

Don't throw away underwear that doesn't fit any more.
Make yourself the ultimate in recycled accessories!

What you will need:

- 1 pair of old, clean, colored underpants
- pins
- needle and colored thread
- 4 old school name tapes or old ribbon
- 3 buttons, same or assorted, at least ³/4 inch across
- 3 old hair ties
- belt for wearing the bag

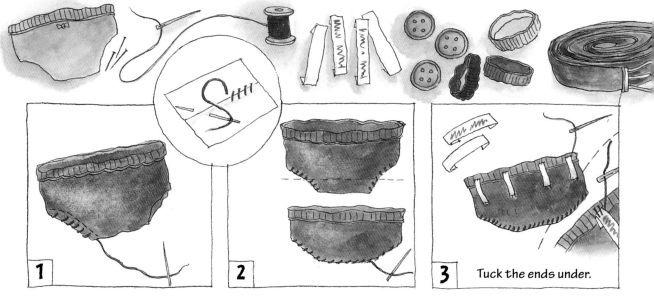

1 Hold the edges of the leg holes together. Pin and sew closed. Knot thread when finished.

2 Fold the gusset of the underwear up inside and oversew closed. Trim off the gusset flap inside.

3 Tuck the ends under.
Turn the underwear over and sew on the name tapes or short lengths of ribbon. These are the belt loops.

78

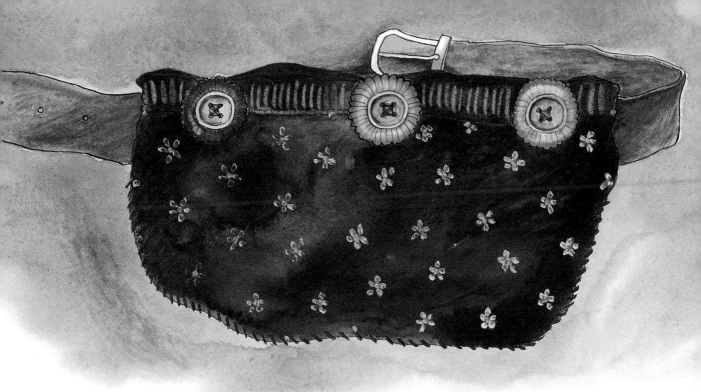

4

Sew the buttons next to the waistband at the front of the underwear.

5

On the back waistband, line up the hair ties with the buttons. Sew them on. Use them to close the bum bag.

6

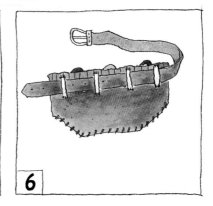

Your fanny pack is ready for action. Just slide a belt through the loops and put it on!

THINK ABOUT IT!

Well-to-do medieval and Tudor folk had a very good use for their old clothes. They cut them into handy little pieces to be used as toilet paper!

Self-portrait with Trash

Make a truly original portrait of yourself. You'll need some of your old clothes that don't fit anymore. You could make portraits of your entire family or some friends too.

What you will need:

- large cardboard box
- pencil
- scissors
- a complete set of old clothes, e.g. tracksuit, T-shirt, socks, etc.
- plastic bags (brown, yellow, black, or orange, depending on your hair color)
- clear tape
- an old cork
- felt-tip pens
- glue
- brown or black wool or old hair ties
- red or pink wool or old hair ties
- old pencil eraser

1

Open up the box and spread it out flat. Lie down on it and ask a friend to draw around your outline.

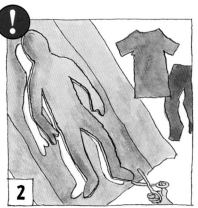

2

Cut out your cardboard self and dress it in your old clothes.

3

Cut strips of the plastic bag. Snip them into fringes for hair. Tape on to the head. Trim to suit your style!

Now create your face.
See the picture for ideas.

Slices of cork colored to match your eyes

Bits of brown or black wool or elastics for eyebrows

Using scissors, shape a nose out of an eraser

Pink or red wool or elastics for mouth

Felt-tip rims and eyelashes

☆☆☆☆☆ **Snazzy Stamp** ☆☆☆☆☆

Wrap masking tape around all but the tip of a potato peeler and use it to gouge out
your own design in an eraser. Then dip the eraser in paint and use it as a stamp.

Wacky Weaving

How many plastic bags have you got lurking around your house? You could transform some of them into this snazzy woven bag. You will need to repeat steps 1 and 2 to make two pieces of weaving.

What you will need:
- 3 different-colored plastic bags, cut into 1 inch wide strips
- medium-sized cardboard box
- scissors
- clear tape

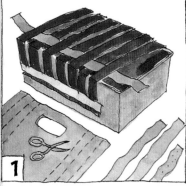

1 Tape strips of one color across the box. Weave strips of other colors in and out across the box.

2 Trim sides, leaving one fringed edge.

Put tape across all the edges of the woven area. Remove from box. Turn over and tape other side. Repeat steps 1 and 2 to make two pieces.

3 Tape 2 pieces of weaving together to form a bag. Snip the fringes into thinner strands.

Tape plastic to table top.

4 Braid 3 strips of plastic. Knot each end to finish. Tape inside bag to form strap.

Onion Fish

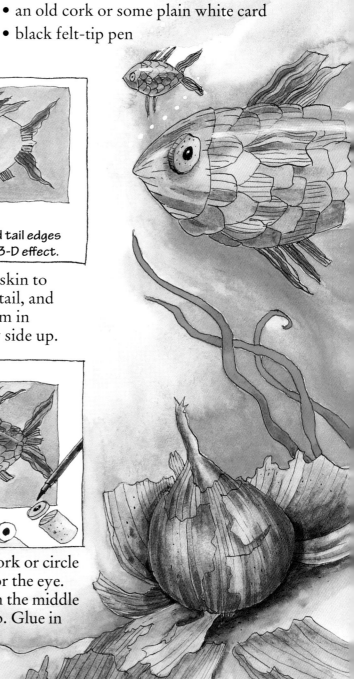

Old onion skins make fantastic fish scales. Collect just the top layer of brown onion skin—you'll see that it's beautifully shiny inside. You could make a whole aquarium!

What you will need:

- colored paper (blue is good)
- pencil
- onion skins
- scissors
- glue
- an old cork or some plain white card
- black felt-tip pen

1 Lightly draw one or more fish outlines on the paper.

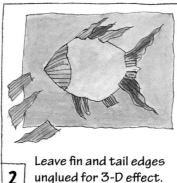

Leave fin and tail edges unglued for 3-D effect.

2 Trim pieces of skin to shape for fins, tail, and head. Glue them in position, shiny side up.

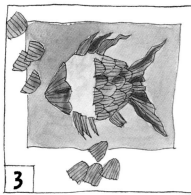

3 Cut scales and glue them on, shiny side up. Start from the tail and overlap them.

4 Cut a slice of cork or circle of cardboard for the eye. Draw a pupil in the middle with the felt-tip. Glue in position.

Big Box Croc

Leave this cardboard critter lying around to surprise your friends. He can be as big as you like—the bigger the better. You can use all those boxes you have been collecting for a rainy day.

What you will need:

- about 8 (or more) assorted rectangular or square boxes, e.g. shoeboxes, tissue boxes, tea boxes, long thin boxes used for packing bottles
- 5 egg cartons
- cardboard from cereal box or similar
- glue
- clear tape
- thick paint (green, white, yellow, black)
- paintbrushes
- string
- scissors
- metal skewer
- pencil

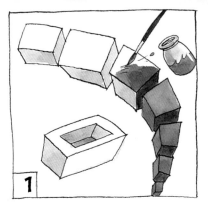

1

For the body: lay all the boxes in a line, with the thinnest ones at the tail. Remove the lids or cut a hole in each box, so you can put your hand inside. Paint the boxes green.

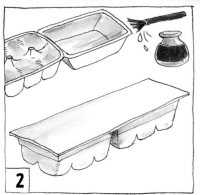

2

For the head: glue 2 of the egg cartons shut. Lay them end to end and cut a rectangle of cardboard to cover the top. Glue it in place.

3

Repeat step 2 with 2 other egg cartons. Cut 2 cups from the last egg carton. Glue them to the top of one head section.

THINK ABOUT IT!

Crocodiles have been around for nearly 200 million years, but they're now endangered because the swamplands and rainforests they live in are being destroyed. Hunters also killed about 10 million crocodiles between 1870 and 1970 to make belts, shoes, bags, and wallets from their skins.

4 *Glue teeth together.*

5

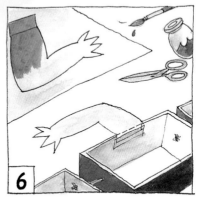

6

Paint the teeth white and the rest of the head green. Leave to dry, then glue the 2 head sections together. paint 2 yellow eyes with black pupils.

With the skewer, make a small hole in each end of all the boxes. Thread a short length of string between each box and the next. Knot the ends inside.

Draw 2 pairs of legs on the cardboard. Paint green, leave to dry, then cut out. Fold a small flap at the end of each limb. Tape firmly inside the body boxes.

Masterful Masks

Elephant Ears

A very simple idea which just uses old egg cartons and cardboard.

What you will need:
- 2 egg carton lids
- grey paint and paintbrush
- scissors
- clear tape
- thin cardboard from cereal box or similar
- pencil
- elastic

1

First paint the lids grey. (Some egg cartons are already gray so this may not be necessary.)

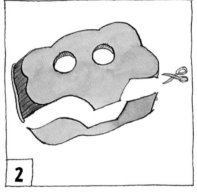

2

Cut 2 eyeholes in one lid. Cut away one edge, as shown, to make head shape and the start of the trunk.

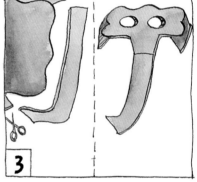

3

Cut a strip from along one side and corner of the other lid to make a trunk. Tape to head.

Paint ears gray if necessary.

4

Draw 2 ear shapes on the cardboard. Cut out and tape to the side of the head with the gray side facing out.

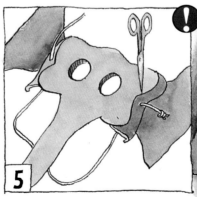

5

Make a hole in each side of the head with the point of the scissors. Thread through elastic and knot to finish.

Foxy Features

Make a cheeky, foxy face using cardboard and old sponges. You could also try out other animals—rabbits, badgers, bears—using the same basic idea.

What you will need:
- cardboard from cereal box or similar
- pencil
- scissors
- wax crayons
- toilet paper tube
- old, clean sponge (yellow, orange, or white)
- glue
- elastic

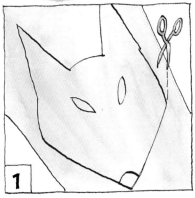

1 Draw a simple fox face on the cardboard. Cut it out. Cut 2 eye holes. Color orange with a black nose.

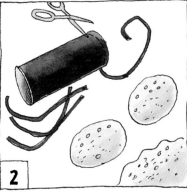

2 Color the toilet paper tube black. Cut 6 very thin strands for whiskers. Cut 2 small cheeks from sponge.

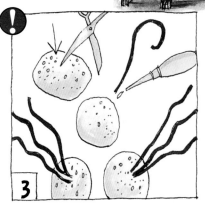

3 Make a hole in each sponge. Dab glue at the end of each whisker, and push 3 into each cheek.

4 Glue the cheeks onto the face. Make 2 holes for the elastic. Thread through and knot to finish.

Crazy Cuttings!

The perfect way to use up old, unwanted family photos once the best ones are in the album. Recycle those old postcards and magazines that are gathering dust too.

What you will need:

- old family photos, especially ones including your mug
- old magazines (sports or music)
- old postcards
- scissors
- glue

WARNING!
Please make sure the photos are not prized family portraits before you start hacking into them!

1 Cut out the heads from the photos. Trim to remove as much background as possible.

2 Sift through postcards for scenes with people in them. Sort through the magazines to find your favorite stars.

3 Now start placing the photo heads on top of the heads in the postcards and magazine pictures to see which ones look best!

THINK ABOUT IT!

Most paper collected for recycling is made into . . . more paper—everything from elegant stationery to toilet paper and cardboard boxes. But amazingly it may also end up as fuel, building materials, cars, shoes, or even kitty litter!

4

Glue them in place. Cut out the magazine pictures.

You can stick your sneaky pictures on your wall or send them to a friend. Autograph your "fan" shots and personalize with a message from the famous "you."

You're Framed!

You could make a simple frame from old pieces of cardboard.

backing cardboard

front piece

Paint cardboard pieces, or cover them with old wrapping paper or foil. Glue together on 3 sides only. Leave one side open to slide in your cool creation.

Jurassock Park

Create your own dinosaurs out of old socks and scourers. The following are just some ideas to get you started. You can make up your own prehistoric pets too!

What you will need:
- clean, old socks, any size or color, though black, green, gray, and brown are best
- ordinary or fluorescent felt-tip pens
- toilet paper tube
- scissors
- used but clean sponges and scourers
- needle and thread
- old red or pink ribbon

Try different-shaped eyeballs and pupils.

1 Put the sock on your hand, with your thumb in the heel. Draw eyes and nostrils in felt-tip pen.

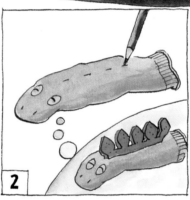

2 Make small felt-tip marks where you would like to position spines, horns, and other features.

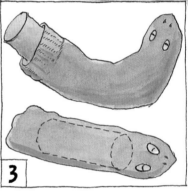

3 Take off the sock and push the toilet paper tube inside it to stop you from sewing right through the sock.

Top Triceratops

Cut a frill out of a large, stiff, green pan scourer. Cut 3 horns from the same scourer. Sew into position using simple running stitches.

Stegosockus

Cut 2 rows of bony plates out of a stiff scourer. Sew in position.

Mighty Meat-eater

Cut some rows of teeth out of a sponge scourer and stitch them inside the mouth. Cut a tongue out of ribbon and stitch in position.

☆☆☆☆☆ Puppet Pets ☆☆☆☆☆

Socks can be made into all kinds of weird and amazing puppet creatures. Just look at your trash collection and see what else you can use: old wool, string, or strips of plastic bag for fur or a mane; can tabs for scales; beads and buttons for eyes.

On Guard!

Save up as much old tinfoil as you can to make your own medieval armor. Design your own emblem for the shield using any old ribbons, colored cardboard, or old glitzy wrapping paper that you can find.

Shiny Shield

Clear tape doesn't show up on tinfoil, so it doesn't matter how many pieces you have to use to cover the shield.

What you will need:
- large piece of cardboard
- pencils and scissors
- old, clean tinfoil
- clear tape
- decorations for emblem

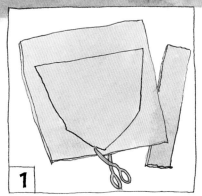

1 Draw the outline of your shield on the cardboard. Cut it out. Cut out a wide strip of cardboard too.

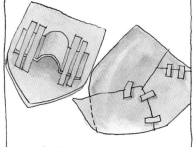

Tuck and tape the edges around the back.

2 Tape the strip on to the back of the shield as shown. Cover the front of the shield with pieces of tinfoil.

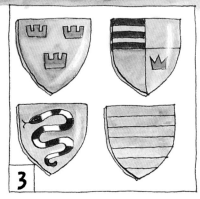

3 Add your own personal emblem to finish.

Short Sword

If you find a large enough piece of cardboard you can make this a long jousting sword instead!

1 Draw the shape of the sword blade on the cardboard. Cut it out.

What you will need:
- thick cardboard
- pencil
- scissors
- old, clean foil pan
- old, clean tinfoil
- clear tape

2 Cut a wide strip from the foil pan. Fold over and tape along the cut edges.

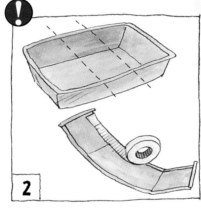

3 Cover the blade with tinfoil. Cut a slit in the middle of the foil strip and slot the blade through. Fix with clear tape. Curve the strip to form the sword hilt.

THINK ABOUT IT!

Medieval muck left behind in the ancient trash pits of castles can give us a perfect picture of what life might have been like then. For example, animal bones tell us what people ate.

Megga Mosaics

You can make mosaics from all kinds of trash—just look at your collection of stuff and try out different materials. Simple patterns, flags, and heraldic emblems all make great designs. You could make yourself a mosaic bedroom nameplate.

Terracotta Eggshells

Collect empty eggshells from cooking or from boiled-egg meals. Wash them out and leave to dry. Six half shells will be enough to make a picture about 6 inches long and 5 1/2 inches wide.

What you will need:
- eggshells
- different-colored paints
- paintbrushes
- paper
- pencil
- glue

| You don't need to paint right to the edge of the shells. | Try a rough version first using colored pencils. | Nip the edges of the shells with your nails to shape them. |

1 Paint some of the eggshells different colors. Leave to dry. Leave some shells unpainted.

2 Draw your design on the paper lightly in pencil. Decide where you want each color to go.

3 Break off bits of shell and apply glue. Press into position. The eggshell will crack, but the inside "skin" will hold it together.

☆☆☆☆☆ **The Finishing Touch** ☆☆☆☆☆

Varnish your mosaic for a real glazed look. Mix 1 teaspoon of Elmer's glue with 3 teaspoons of water and brush lightly across the mosaic. It will become clear when dry.

Magazine Mosaic

Sort through old magazines and catalogs and look for solid blocks of color. You will need about four different colors to work with. Slightly different shades of the same color are fine. Clothing catalogs are really good for solid areas of one color.

What you will need:
- old magazines or catalogs
- scissors and glue
- plain paper and pencil
- envelopes or plastic pots to keep colored squares separate

1

Cut out solid areas of your chosen colors and trim down to ½ inch squares.

2

Draw your design in pencil first.

Do the background last.

3

Glue a small area of the outline at a time and fill in with squares. Where whole squares will not fit, cut them to fill the space.

THINK ABOUT IT!

Roman public lavatories were often decorated with mosaics, and dolphin designs were very popular. At the Roman bathrooms in Timgad, in North Africa, carved dolphin armrests were even placed between each seat!

Fit for a Pharaoh

This is really royal trash and guaranteed to impress your friends.

Jeweled Collar

Ask your friends to help you collect loads of can tabs. You will need as many different colors as possible for the jewels!

What you will need:
- an old T-shirt (any color)
- colored pencils and paper
- pinking shears
- can tabs
- needle and thread

1 Draw the outline of the collar on the T-shirt. Cut it out with pinking shears.

2 Place lines of can tabs in a pattern on the front of the collar. Copy your design on a piece of paper.

3 Sew the can tabs onto the collar with a simple running stitch. To wear the collar, just pull it on over your head.

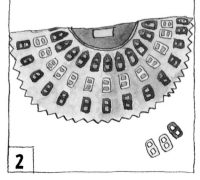

Amulet Armlet

Wear this embossed armlet on your upper arm in true Ancient Egyptian style. The eye design is the Eye of Horus—the protective sign of the sky god! Try some designs of your own.

What you will need:
- 1 toilet paper tube
- scissors
- thick string or old shoelace
- glue
- old tinfoil (silver or gold, but clean)

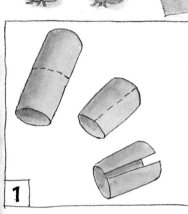

1 Cut the tube in half. Make a vertical cut up one of the halves.

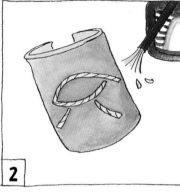

2 Glue on pieces of string or shoelace in an eye design as shown. Let it dry.

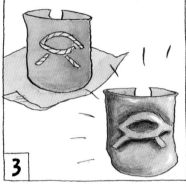

3 Carefully cover the tube with a piece of foil. Gently press around the eye design.

THINK ABOUT IT!

Unfortunately Ancient Egyptian mummies have not always been treated with respect. Ground-up mummy used to be made into medicines during the sixteenth and seventeenth centuries.

The Great Garbage Race

A silly game for two or more players. The loser gets a wonderful, mucky surprise! This is definitely one for outdoors.

Each player has to walk the course in bare feet. Everyone else closes their eyes and listens. The player must try not to rustle, clank, or squeal with disgust. Whoever is noisiest has to get inside the garbage bag and jump along the course to gather up the trash afterwards.

What you will need:
- old newspapers
- 9 unsquashed, empty drink cans
- a few banana skins or a pile of potato, carrot, or other vegetable peelings
- several empty chip packets
- some polystyrene fruit and vegetable trays
- 1 large garbage bag or plastic refuse sack

3 towers of drink cans. (Leave just a few inches between each one.)

old newspapers

a pile of peelings

polystyrene trays

chip packets

more newspaper

THINK ABOUT IT!
The highest point on Staten Island near New York is a mountain of trash from the city. Do you know where your garbage ends up when you throw it in the trash can?

98

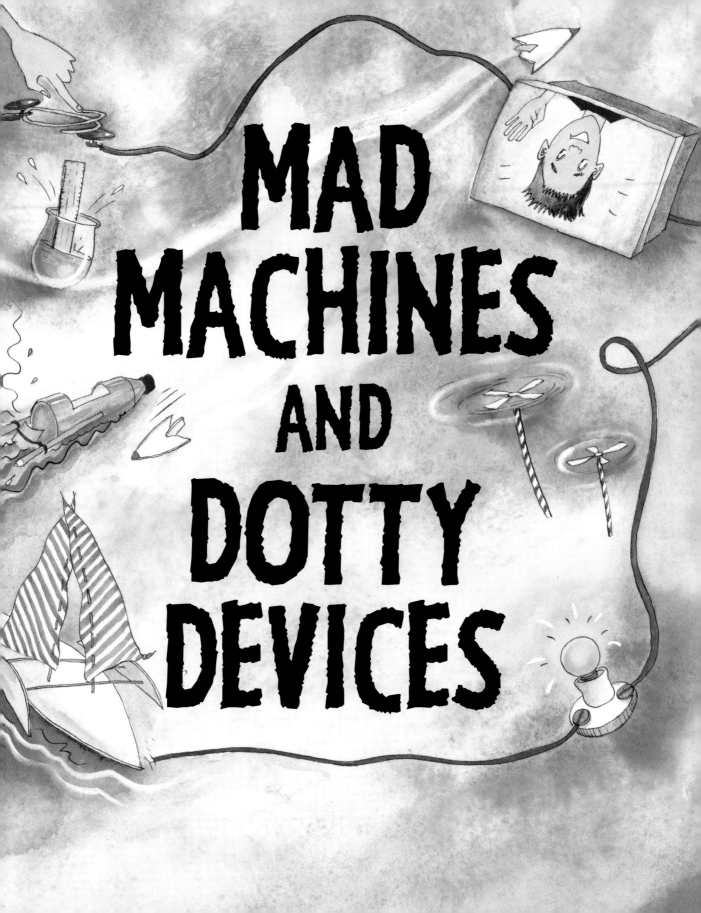

Before You Begin

Most of the contraptions in this book are made with old stuff you will have around the house already. Don't forget to cover work surfaces with newspaper before you start, and clean up afterwards!

For the Whizzy Whirler on page 120 you will need to trace the template on to a piece of cardboard. This is how to do it:

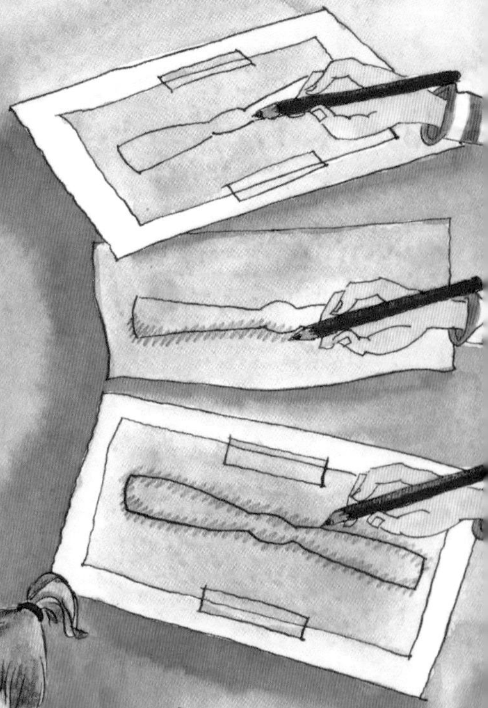

1 Trace the template shape using tracing paper, masking tape, and a pencil.

2 Turn over the tracing paper and scribble over the lines with the pencil.

3 Turn the paper over again and tape it onto the card. Retrace over the lines.

boxes

plastic bottles

clear tape

cardboard

polystyrene packing material

paper fasteners

paper clips

straws

reusable
sticky tack

thumbtacks

string and
thread

toilet paper tubes

balloons

electrical wire

glue

cardboard

rubber bands

old jam jars

marbles

clothespins

paper

mirrors

scissors

tracing paper

You will need a bit of grown-up help
in one or two places. These have been
marked with this special symbol.

101

Air Power

Blast Off!

This balloon rocket really whizzes along. You can use the same balloon again and again to show it off to your friends. You'll need a friend standing by to help set up the launch.

What you will need:
- 7 feet of string
- drinking straw
- chair
- balloon
- clear tape
- clothespin

1 Thread the straw on to the string. Tie one end to a door handle and the other to a chair.

2 Place the chair so that the string is taut. Blow up the balloon and pin it closed.

3 Get a friend to help you tape the balloon on to the straw. Now unpin the balloon and watch it go!

It's a Fact!

Isaac Newton's Third Law of Motion says that for every action there is an equal and opposite reaction. In this case, the air is pushed out of the back of the balloon and this "action" makes the balloon move forwards, the "opposite reaction."

In a real rocket, fuel burns and makes hot gases, which come rushing out of the back of the engine. This propels the rocket upwards.

You could tape a small box under the balloon for carrying "cargo"—an empty matchbox is ideal.

Funky Fountains

Here are some fun fountains to make with your friends. Make a few and have a competition to see whose is best. You could add some food coloring to the water for extra fun. It's a good idea to do this outside!

What you will need:
- large, empty, plastic drink bottle
- 2 bendy drinking straws
- Plasticine or reusable sticky tack

1

Remove any labels from the bottle. Half-fill the bottle with water.

2

Put one straw into the water and position the other one so it is just above the water. Put some Plasticine or sticky tack tightly round the mouth to make an airtight seal.

3

Blow!

Put the bottle into a sink or take it outside. Now blow into the straw that is not in the water.

See how powerful air can be by blowing through a straw at a paper boat!

Rocket Man

Wernher von Braun (1912–1977) was a German inventor who longed to send a rocket to the moon. Unfortunately, during the Second World War (1939–1945) he was ordered to design rocket bombs instead. After the war he went to work in America and by the 1960s he was working at NASA (the US space program). He led the team that launched the Saturn rockets that first took men to the moon.

It's a Fact!

When you blow air through a straw it squashes the air up—or compresses it. This makes the air more powerful. The air you blow into the bottle squashes up in the space above the water too and pushes the water up through the other straw.

Mighty Robot

Although this robot friend will not do chores for you or clean up your room, he's fun to have around and will hold stuff for you. You can really go to town when adding buttons and features to your robot. These are just some ideas to get you started.

What you will need:
- 1 medium-sized box
- 1 small box
- aluminum foil
- clear tape
- 6 toilet paper tubes
- scissors
- 3 glittery pipe cleaners
- sequins
- glue
- old pieces of polystyrene packing
- small bottle or carton lids
- old, shiny candy wrappers

1

Cover both the boxes with foil as if you were wrapping a present. Use clear tape to secure the foil.

2

Cover 4 of the toilet paper tubes with foil and tuck the foil inside the ends.

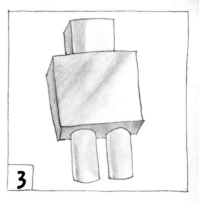

3

Tape the small box on top of the medium one. Then tape 2 of the covered tubes underneath for legs.

It's a Fact!

Robots are used in many industries on factory production lines. But they don't look at all like the artificial humans (androids) you see in films! They're really useful, though, and can do the jobs that humans would find very boring. In car manufacturing, robots weld together the steel panels to make the car body and then spray the body with several coats of paint.

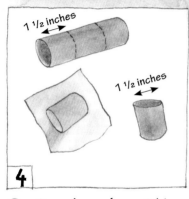

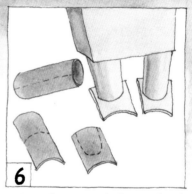

4

Cut 2 sections about 1 1/2 inch long from the ends of a remaining tube. Cover these with foil. Tuck in the ends.

5

Tape these on to the other 2 covered tubes to form "hands." Now tape these "arms" on to the robot's body.

6

Cut the remaining tube in half lengthways. Cut 2 "feet" as shown. Cover these with foil. Tape on to the legs.

7 With adult help, use the scissors to pierce 3 holes in the top of the head.

8 Curl the pipe cleaners around your finger and then push them through the holes.

9 Glue on sequins for eyes. Cover a piece of rectangular polystyrene with foil and stick it on to make a mouth.

10 Cover lids with foil and candy wrappers and stick on for buttons.

11 Use the arms and hands to keep pens, torches, hairbrushes, or even your toothbrush tidy!

Androids in the Future?

Scientists are researching ways of making robots that can think for themselves and not have to be programmed before they perform certain tasks. Maybe one day you might have a robot around the house who will clean without having to be nagged!

Spyscope

Make a nifty periscope for peering over the fence at your neighbors! The sort of mirrors you need are small makeup ones, which you can get from dollar stores or pharmacies.

What you will need:
- 1 long, thin box about 9 ½ inches long and 2 inches wide
- scissors and clear tape

- 2 small rectangular mirrors about 2 inches x 3 inches

WARNING
Never point the Spyscope at the sun or you could damage your eyes.

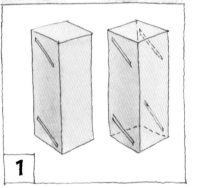

1 Cut 2 slanting slits on one side of the box. Turn it over and cut 2 more. These should line up with the first slits.

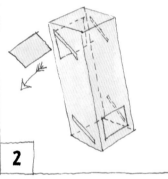

2 Cut 2 square windows in the box, as shown. They should line up with the slits.

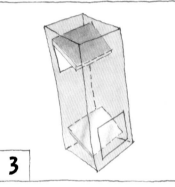

3 Slide the mirrors through the slits so that their reflective sides are facing each other. Use tape to secure them if necessary.

4 Hold one window to your face and look through. What can you see?

It's a Fact!

Light reflects, or bounces, from the top mirror to the bottom mirror. When you point the top mirror at something or someone, the light bouncing from it will then bounce down to the bottom mirror into your eyes and you will be able to see it!

Up Periscope!

Submarines use periscopes as their "eyes." Modern submarines have some really amazing periscopes with all kinds of special equipment. "Attack" periscopes are really narrow at the top so that they cannot be seen by enemy radar. "Search" periscopes are decked out with cameras and night vision so that they can even be used when it's dark.

Anchors Aweigh!

Make yourself a speedy trimaran that will skim along in a breeze! You need to use the templates on the inside front cover. You could try making other boats too—maybe a catamaran with 2 hulls instead of 3.

What you will need:

- 1 large polystyrene circle used for packing pizzas (wiped clean)
- tracing paper and pencil
- scissors
- clear tape
- 4 wooden skewers about 10 inches long
- 9 1/2 inches x 5 inches piece of very thin fabric or a clean, disposable cleaning cloth
- thread

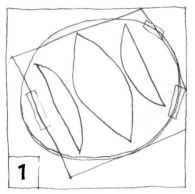

1 Trace the hull templates. Trace the side hull twice. Tape the tracing paper onto the polystyrene. Cut through the paper and polystyrene.

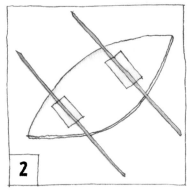

2 Remove the tracing paper. Tape 2 skewers across the center of the main hull.

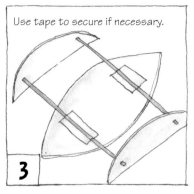

Use tape to secure if necessary.

3 Hold the side hulls with their curved sides upwards and gently push them on to the ends of the skewers.

4 Cut the fabric or cloth into 2 triangles. Thread a skewer up the side of each one. Tie an 8-inch length of thread to each loose corner.

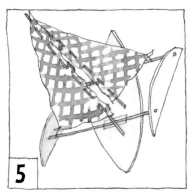

5 Push these "masts" into the main hull. Tie the loose threads to the horizontal skewers.

6 Tape the 2 masts together at the top. You're ready to sail!

Monohulls and Hydrofoils

"Drag" is the force that slows a boat down when it's moving through the water. The less hull a boat has in the water, the faster it can go.

A monohull is a boat with one hull. A normal sailing yacht is a monohull and can sail at up to 20 miles per hour.

A catamaran has two hulls. When the wind blows strongly it can lean and balance on one hull and go at up to 35 miles per hour.

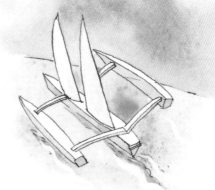

A trimaran has three hulls—one main hull and two "floats." In high winds it can speed along on one float at up to 37 1/2 miles per hour.

A hydrofoil has three hulls and amazing slanting runners under the side hulls. When the wind gets up, all three hulls can be lifted out of the water and the boat speeds along on these runners at up to 40 miles per hour.

Weather Station

Be a weather scientist with this handy barometer and rain gauge. The barometer will tell you what the air pressure is like and you'll be able to see how this affects whether it rains or not! Why not keep a record of your findings in a notebook?

Beaker Barometer

If you can't find clear tubing or straws then use a regular stripy straw—the food coloring will help you to see the level of the water.

What you will need:
- clear glass or plastic beaker or jam jar
- clear tape and ruler
- 8 inch clear plastic tube or drinking straw
- food coloring
- reusable sticky tack

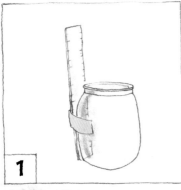

1

Tape the ruler upright on the outside of the beaker or jar.

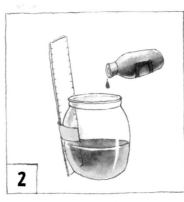

2

Half-fill the beaker or jar with cold water and put a few drops of food coloring in it.

3

Tape the tube or straw to the inside of the jar. It should not touch the bottom.

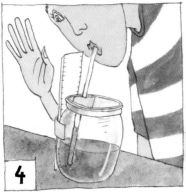

4

Suck some water halfway up the tube. Pinch the tube. Cap the top with sticky tack.

Keep your barometer indoors, but make sure it is not in a drafty or sunny place. Note the level of the water in the tube each day, and note if the weather changes.

Rain Catcher

This rain gauge can be hung up over a fence or balcony. Make sure it isn't underneath any overhanging bits of building or roof, or under any trees. Note the level of the water each day in your notebook.

What you will need:

- clean, empty jam jar (preferably with straight sides) or half a clear plastic bottle
- plastic ruler
- reusable sticky tack
- old wire coat hanger

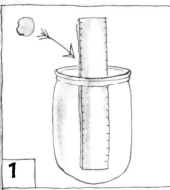

1 Place the ruler inside the jar or bottle half. Secure it to the side of the jar with the sticky tack.

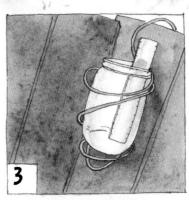

2 Ask a grown-up to help you untwist the wire coat hanger and then curl it around the jar or bottle.

3 Make sure the wire goes underneath the jar or bottle. Finish off with a curl that you can use to hang up the rain gauge.

It's a Fact!

How does your beaker barometer work?

When the pressure in the atmosphere goes up, the water in the barometer jar is forced downwards. This will push the water in the tube or straw upwards. You will see that happening if you check the level against the ruler. Rising atmospheric pressure means that we should have clear or sunny weather.

If the water in the tube is going down this is because the air pressure is going down and could be bringing with it some cloudy or rainy weather.

Snap Happy

See how a camera works by making this simple device. You'll need a friend to help you.

What you will need:
- old shoebox or similar
- thick black paint and paintbrush
- pin
- tracing paper
- scissors
- clear tape
- large, adult-sized coat

Don't make hole too big.

1 Take the lid off the box. Paint the inside black and leave it to dry. Use the pin to make a hole in the middle of the bottom of the box.

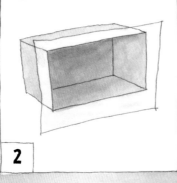

2 Cut out a large piece of tracing paper to fit across the open side of the box with about an inch to spare on all sides.

3 Tape the paper firmly around all the sides of the box so that it is stretched tightly across the open side.

Camera Obscura

Camera obscura means "dark chamber" in Latin. The pinhole camera is a camera obscura on a small scale. But did you know that whole rooms can be made into dark chambers? Artists and astronomers over the centuries have observed images from the outside world through a pinhole of light coming into a specially darkened room.

4 Now you are ready to try out your "camera." Take the box and coat outside because it works best in bright light. (If you are inside, point it towards a light or lamp.)

7 Point the pinhole side of the box at a building or a tree or some other object and you will see an upside-down image of it on the paper screen!

6 Ask a friend to help put the coat over your head and around the sides and bottom of the box. No light should get in!

5 Hold the box to your eyes with the tracing paper facing you. Don't press it up to your face, though.

It's a Fact!

Rays of light bounce off the object at which you are pointing the pinhole. These rays carry a picture of it through the pinhole. As these light rays come through the hole they cross over, and so your picture appears upside-down. This is how real cameras see pictures too, except they have film inside them instead of tracing paper! Your eye is just like a pinhole camera. Luckily your brain unscrambles the pictures you see so that they are the right way up.

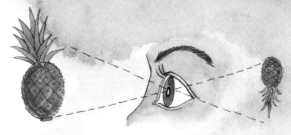

Paddle Power

This wacky, whizzy paddleboat will make bath time much more fun! You will need to try and find two old pens which are of similar length and weight. Paddle power is another way of seeing Newton's Third Law of Motion in action (see page 102).

What you will need:

- 1 small, empty, plastic bottle with lid
- scissors
- 2 old ballpoint or felt-tip pens
- clear tape
- elastic band

1

Cut a section out of the bottle as shown. Do not throw away the bit you have cut out.

2

Tape the pens to the sides of the bottle. Half of each one should stick out beyond the end of the bottle.

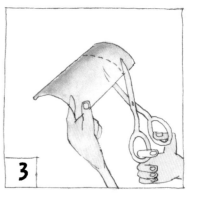

3

Cut a piece of plastic from the strip you have kept. It should be as long as the pen ends and just a bit narrower than the gap between them.

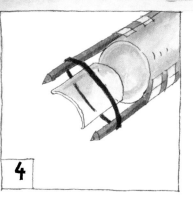

4

Put the elastic band around the pen ends. Place the plastic piece through it with the curved edge facing down.

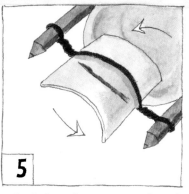

5

Wind the plastic round and round in a counterclockwise direction. Twist it as far as it will go.

6

Put the boat in a bath of water and let it go!

Wheels in the Water

Steam engines for ships were first used in paddleboats. The engine turned two massive paddle wheels. The trouble was that these paddle steamers were not much good on the open sea. When there was rough weather the waves lifted one wheel out of the water while the other one was completely submerged. This strained the engine badly. When propellers were invented, they were used instead of the paddle wheels because they didn't waste so much of the engine's energy.

Chocks Away!

You could make a few of these cool catapult contraptions and race them with your friends. You'll need to trace the templates on the inside back cover. You can experiment with different-shaped wings, so feel free to adapt these!

What you will need:
- 1 large polystyrene circle used for packing pizzas (wiped clean)
- tracing paper and pencil
- clear tape
- scissors
- glue or double-sided tape
- 1 paper fastener
- reusable sticky tack
- elastic band

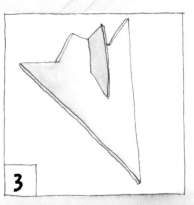

1 Trace the 3 template shapes. Tape the tracing paper on to the polystyrene.

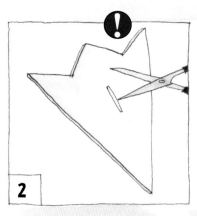

2 Cut through both paper and polystyrene. Cut a slit in the main body as marked on the template.

3 Push the tail piece through the slit so that it stands upright.

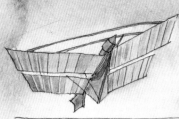

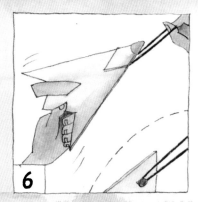

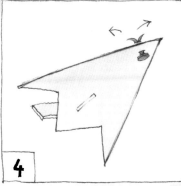

4

Push the paper fastener through the main body near the "nose." Fold the "legs" of the fastener back but make sure the pinhead is not too tight up against the polystyrene.

5

Using glue or double-sided tape, fix the small body piece on top of the fastener. Mold a piece of sticky tack around the glider's nose to weight it.

6

Place the elastic band around the head of the fastener. Pull it tight and launch your glider (let go of the tail!)

The Wonderful Wright Brothers

The first people to create a flying machine with an engine—
Wilbur and Orville Wright—started with gliders!
They created some amazing contraptions.
Some of them travelled up to 650 feet but they relied
on the wind for power.

The ingenious Wright brothers eventually came up
with a flying machine with an engine and two propellers.
On December 17th, 1903, it took off and flew about 130 feet.
It was the world's first powered flight.

Manic Messages

Build a nifty electrical circuit with two switches to control the flashing bulbs and send messages by Morse code. The complete code is on the opposite page. Send a friend into the next room with their half of the circuit. To receive a message, you need to hold down your switch while your friend taps their switch off and on to make the bulbs flash. Then you send your answer while your friend holds their switch down.

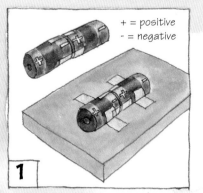

+ = positive
- = negative

1 Tape the batteries into 2 pairs (put the + and - together as shown). Tape them on to the box lids or cardboard.

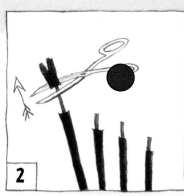

2 Using the scissors, strip a small bit of plastic from each end of all the pieces of wire.

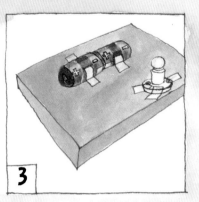

3 Tape the bulb-holders onto the lids or cardboard and screw in the bulbs.

WARNING!
You must NEVER experiment or play with AC power, the electricity from an electrical socket.

5 Fix each end of one 6 ½ foot wire to the batteries with the sticky tack or Plasticine.

close-up of switch

switch

6 Use sticky tack or Plasticine to fix one 5 inch wire to each of the other ends of the batteries. Curl the other end around a thumbtack, and push it through a paper clip and into the cardboard.

7 Curl each end of the other 6 ½ foot wire under one screw of each bulb-holder and tighten the screws.

What you will need:

- 2 shoe-box lids or pieces of thick cardboard
- 4 x 1.5 volt batteries
- 2 x 2–2.5 v flashlight bulbs and holders
- 1 ½ x 5 inch lengths of plastic-covered electrical wire
- 2 x 6 ½ foot lengths of plastic-covered electrical wire
- scissors
- reusable sticky tack or Plasticine
- clear tape
- screwdriver
- 4 thumbtacks
- 2 paper clips

4

Use the screwdriver to loosen the screws on each side of the bulb-holders.

Dots and Dashes

Morse code was invented in 1838 by Samuel Morse. He sent a message in the form of electrical signals along a wire. He tapped out long and short sounds to represent different letters of the alphabet. You can do the same by making the light bulbs flash quickly for a dot or longer for a dash.

A • —
B — • • •
C — • — •
D — • •
E •
F • • — •
G — — •
H • • • •
I • •
J • — — —
K — • —
L • — • •
M — —
N — •
O — — —
P • — — •
Q — — • —
R • — •
S • • •
T —
U • • —
V • • • —
W • — —
X — • • —
Y — • — —
Z — — • •

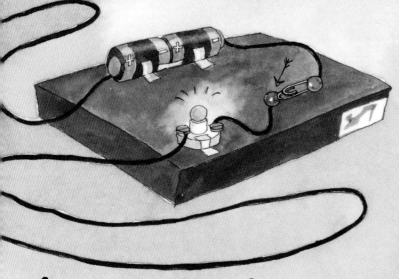

8 Curl the end of a 5 inch wire around a thumbtack and then push it into the cardboard.

9 Curl the other end of the 5 inch wire under the screws on the other sides of the bulb-holders.

Whizzy Whirler

This is a simple version of a helicopter! Follow the instructions on page 100 to trace the template from the inside front cover onto the cardboard.

What you will need:
- thin cardboard (from a cereal box or similar)
- tracing paper and pencil
- scissors
- drinking straw
- paper clip
- clear tape

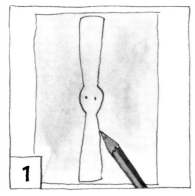

1 Trace the template outline onto the card. Cut it out.

2 Uncurl the paper clip so that it just has one bend left. Push the ends through the dots in the middle of the propeller.

3 Push the ends down into the straw. Use clear tape to make the propeller extra secure.

4 Hold the straw between the palms of your hands. Roll the straw between them and then let it go with a throwing motion.

It's a Fact!

Squashed or compressed air helps a helicopter take off. As the blades, or rotors, whiz around they push air down. This squashes the air underneath them, and this compressed air pushes the helicopter upwards.

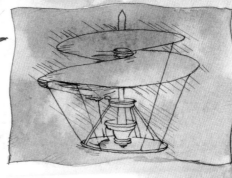

The Ingenious Leonardo

An amazing, early version of a helicopter was designed by Leonardo da Vinci during the fifteenth century. He was a painter, architect, musician, and inventor who drew all sorts of designs for many weird and wonderful devices. His "airscrew" was a corkscrew-shaped contraption. The screw turning would have made it climb upwards like a modern-day helicopter.

Sikorsky's Solution

The first helicopter was invented in 1907 by a Frenchman named Paul Cornu. It had two rotors, and could go up about 6 ½ feet into the air. The trouble was that the body of the helicopter spun round too—in the opposite direction to the wings!

This problem is known as "torque."

In 1939 a Russian called Igor Sikorsky designed a helicopter with a main rotor and one at the tail of the machine too. This small rotor solved the problem of "torque" and kept the body of the helicopter from whirling around at the same time as the wings!

Kinetic Capers

A fun and wacky game for two. Make a mad marble run with two columns of toilet paper tubes! The first marble to finish is the winner.

What you will need:
- thin cardboard (from a cereal box or similar)
- 8 toilet paper tubes
- pencil
- scissors
- clear tape
- a very large sheet of thick cardboard
- double-sided tape
- marbles

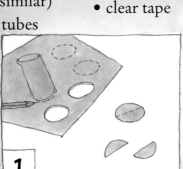

1 Draw 5 circles on the thin cardboard using a tube as a guide. Cut these circles out and then cut them in half.

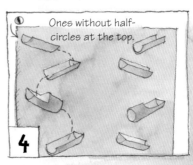

4 like this

4 like this

2 Cut 4 of the toilet paper tubes in half lengthways. Cut the remaining 4 as shown.

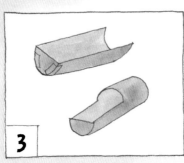

3 Put 2 halves to one side. Tape a half-circle of cardboard to one end of all the other halved or cut rolls.

Ones without half-circles at the top.

4 Use double-sided tape to stick the rolls on to the large piece of cardboard as shown.

It's a Fact!

When you let the marbles go at the top of the "run," they run down because of the pull of gravity. At the top of the run, before you let them go, the marbles are full of "potential" energy. Once they are rolling down this energy becomes "kinetic" energy.

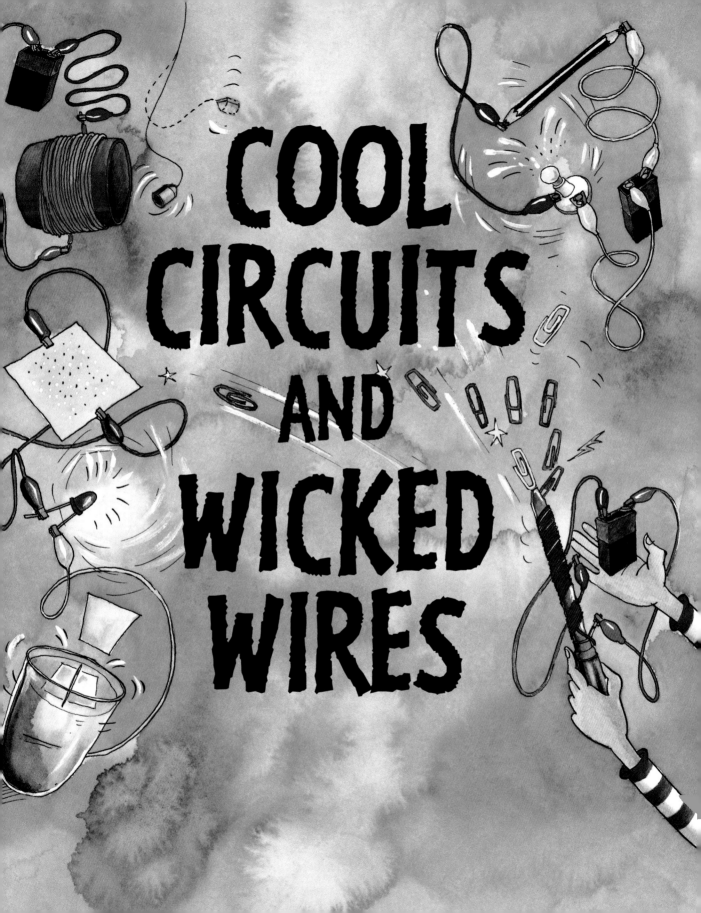

Before You Begin

Most of these experiments give you pretty immediate and wicked results. Some of them take a little longer and need more patience, but they are worth it!

You will be using lots of household items like salt, water, plastic cups, paper clips, and so on. However, you will also need to buy a few inexpensive things from an electrical or hobby electronic shop (see page 125). The stuff you need to buy is listed on the opposite page.

Read through the whole experiment before you begin. If it doesn't work the first time, try again! Remember that the circuits have to be done exactly like the instructions and pictures in the book. You could keep notes or even draw up your results like a real scientist or inventor.

Remember never to play with AC power in the plugs and sockets and equipment in your house.

Things you'll probably have at home already:

HB pencils
You will need to sharpen these at both ends for the experiments in the book!

Salt

Paper towels

Plastic cups or beakers
You need 5 of these.

Needle

Medium- or large-sized screwdriver with a plastic handle

Bar magnet
This should have N and S marked on it.

Small round magnet

Paper clips

Copper-style coins
(Like pennies)

Aluminum foil

Things to buy:

9-volt PP3 battery
(ordinary small rectangular type)

Crocodile clip leads
You'll need about 7 (try to get red, black, white, yellow, and green, but don't worry if you can't get all those colors).

LED (short for Light Emitting Diode)
Buy the cheapest red one to start with.

Insulated wire
You'll need about 13 feet of this plastic-coated wire—the sort with one wire inside the plastic not lots of very thin wires.

Compass
A small, cheap plastic compass

Flashlight bulb and bulb-holder
Look for a 4.5-volt bulb if possible, but anything from 3 volts to 6 volts will do.

Sticky tack or Plasticine

Clear tape

Scissors

Plastic top from a large aerosol can

Simple Stuff

Electricity flows a bit like water. Water is controlled by putting it through pipes and storing it in tanks. Electricity is controlled by running it through wires and storing it in batteries.

When electricity flows, little packets of electricity called electrons move through the wire. Electrons are very small. You cannot see them, but you can see the effect they have on things. In this simple circuit the little electrons are moving so fast and there are so many of them that they make the bit of wire in the light bulb get hot and glow.

What you will need:
- 1 x 9-volt PP3 battery
- 1 red crocodile clip lead
- 1 black crocodile clip lead
- 1x 4.5-volt flashlight bulb and bulb-holder

1

Screw the flashlight bulb into the bulb-holder.

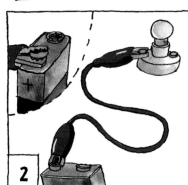

2

Clip one end of the red lead to the positive (+) side of the battery. Clip the other end to one side of the bulb-holder.

3

Clip one end of the black lead to the negative (-) side of the battery.

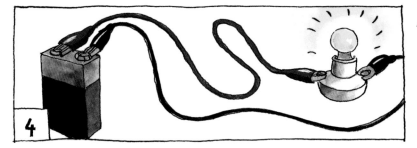

4

Clip the other end of the black lead to the remaining free end of the bulb-holder and see the bulb light up!

Croc Clips
It doesn't matter what color the crocodile clip leads are, really. It just helps us to explain what you need to do!

Watch out! They can nip!

Batteries

Batteries have a positive (+) and a negative (-) side. These sides are called terminals.

Bright Spark

The first electric lightbulb was invented in America by Thomas Edison in October 1879. As a boy he had been expelled from school because the headmaster thought he was stupid! By the time he was ten years old Edison had set up his own laboratory and, in years to come, he would also invent the world's first machine for recording sounds.

The Electrons

Electrons are little packets of negative electricity. This means that they flow from the negative (-) side of the battery to the positive (+) side through the circuit. Electrons are attracted by positive things. The amount of force that the electrons flow with is measured in volts. That is why we talk about the voltage of a battery.

I'm feeling very negative today.

Pencil Power

What happens if you add a pencil to a circuit? Imagine water flowing through a nice, clear pipe. If you put a bit of sponge in the pipe the water would still be able to go through, but the sponge would slow it down. Well, in our circuit a pencil will do a similar thing to the sponge—it will slow the flow of electrons down. It's what is called a "resistor" in electrical circuits. Resistors make sure just the right amount of electrons are delivered to each part of a circuit inside electronic gadgets like TVs and computers. Without them, it would be like having a faucet either switched off completely, or blasting out water with no way of slowing it down.

What you will need:
- 1x 9-volt PP3 battery
- 1 red crocodile clip lead
- 1 black crocodile clip lead
- 1 green crocodile clip lead
- 1 HB pencil, sharpened at both ends
- 1x 4.5-volt flashlight bulb and bulb-holder

The Electrons

What are the electrons up to in this circuit? In a simple circuit with very low resistance, the electrons can whiz around quite easily. The pencil resistor here is making it more difficult for them. It's as if they have an obstacle in their path. It's like battling through an army obstacle course.

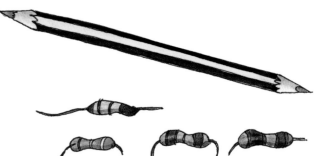

Controlling the Flow

Resistors are all around us! All the electronic stuff in your house will have resistors inside it. Not only are they in all kinds of gadgets, but some of these resistors are even made from the same substance that is inside the pencils we've just used—carbon!

1 Screw the bulb into the bulb-holder.

2 Clip one end of the red lead to the positive (+) side of the battery. Clip the other end to one side of the bulb-holder.

3 *Clip to lead of the pencil.* Clip one end of the black lead to the negative (-) side of the battery. Clip the other end to one end of the pencil.

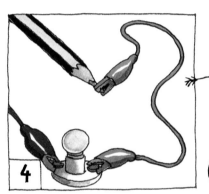

4 Clip the green lead to the other end of the pencil and to the remaining free side of the bulb-holder.

The bulb does not glow as brightly as it did in Simple Stuff. You can test this by removing the pencil and reconnecting the circuit without it.

Wicked Resistors

Now have some fun making different types of circuits using pencil resistors. You can try doing it with more than two pencils each time if you like.

Two is More!

First we're going to use two pencils connected across the circuit. This is what's called a "parallel" circuit.

What you will need:
- 1 x 9-volt PP3 battery

- 7 crocodile clip leads
- 2 HB pencils, sharpened at both ends
- 1 x 4.5-volt flashlight bulb and bulb-holder

Make a junction of clips.

Clip the croc clips to the lead of the pencils.

Bulb and bulb-holder

Make a junction of clips.

The Electrons

The electrons are still having a tricky time battling their way through, but at least they've got two routes to choose from and more of them can complete the course. This means the bulb will shine more brightly.

Two is Less!

Now try making a different sort of circuit with the pencils in line with each other. This is what is called a "series" circuit.

What you will need:
- 1 x 4.5-volt flashlight bulb and bulb-holder
- 1 x 9-volt PP3 battery
- 4 crocodile clip leads
- 2 HB pencils, sharpened at both ends

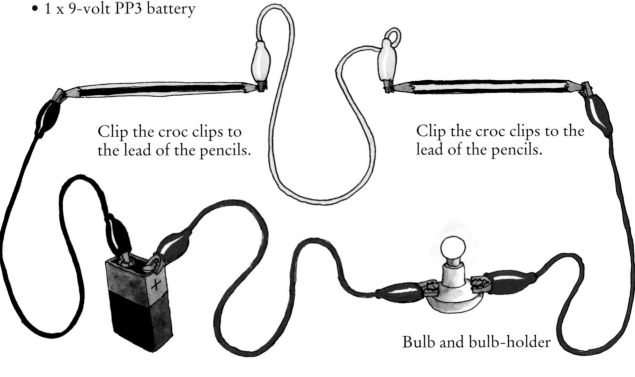

Clip the croc clips to the lead of the pencils.

Clip the croc clips to the lead of the pencils.

Bulb and bulb-holder

The Electrons

This time the electrons are faced with a longer route. They have to try and fight their way through with only one possible path. The bulb will not shine very brightly because not so many of them can get through at a time.

Ohm's Word is Law

Resistance is measured in ohms, named after a German scientist called Georg Simon Ohm. He did a lot of work on electricity but met a lot of resistance from people who didn't think his ideas were all that important!

I just want to go Ohm!

Colorful Circuit

The lightbulb is a fantastic invention, but nowadays it is being replaced in lots of equipment—even flashlights and car headlights—by a special electronic component called a Light Emitting Diode, or LED for short. LEDs are made by an incredibly tricky process that makes the lightbulb look as if it belongs in the Stone Age!

You can buy them quite cheaply in hardware stores and they come in all sorts of colors. The great thing about LEDs is that they don't need much electricity to light them up. In fact, in this circuit, if you didn't have a bit of paper towel to act as a resistor the battery would be too powerful for the LED and it would get zapped!

LEDs have one leg shorter than the other!

positive (+) side

negative (-) side

WARNING!
Do not touch a battery if your hands are wet! It's not that dangerous but it might give you a little bit of an electric shock.

What you will need:
- 1x 9-volt PP3 battery
- 1 red crocodile clip lead
- 1 black crocodile clip lead
- 1 green crocodile clip lead
- ¼ piece paper towel
- 1 LED (any color)

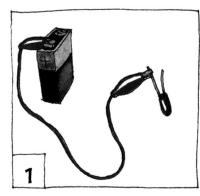

1

Clip one end of the red lead to the positive (+) side of the battery. Clip the other end to the long leg (+) of the LED.

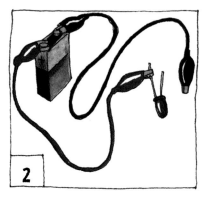

2

Clip one end of the black lead to the negative (-) side of the battery.

3

Fold the piece of paper towel into four.

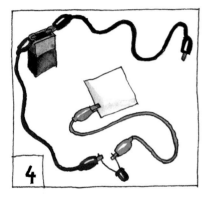 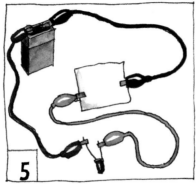 

Clip one end of the green lead to one side of the paper towel. Clip the other end to the short leg (-) of the LED.

Clip the remaining free end of the black lead to the other side of the paper towel.

Sprinkle a little bit of water on the paper towel until it soaks across it. Watch what happens to the LED.

Salty Circuit

Make the same circuit again, but this time sprinkle some salt on the wet paper towel. See what happens to the brightness of the LED.

The Electrons

What do the electrons get up to inside LEDs? When an electric current is running through an LED it's as if the electrons inside it are jumping off a diving board. Instead of making a splash of water, they each give off a splash of light. The voltage from the battery pushes them up to the top of the board and then wheee! They fall down and give off their splash of light. The dry paper towel on its own won't work—it has too high a resistance. But when you sprinkle some water on it, enough electrons can get through to light the LED. If you put salt on the towel as well, even more electrons can pass around the circuit because the salt reduces the resistance of the water, and the LED glows even more brightly.

Briny Battery

You can make your own battery using saltwater and coins! It will produce enough electricity to make an LED work—your cheap red one works best. This simple, homemade battery isn't quite powerful enough to make a flashlight bulb work, which is why LEDs are so handy. They don't use up as much electricity.

What you will need:
- 6 crocodile clip leads
- 1 red LED
- 5 plastic mugs or beakers
- 10 teaspoons salt
- 5 pennies
- 5 squares of aluminum foil, 2 inches x 2 inches

1 Half-fill each plastic mug or beaker with water. Sprinkle 2 teaspoons of salt into each one of them.

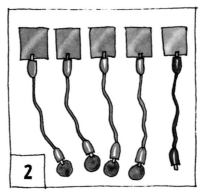

2 Clip a separate lead to each aluminum square. Clip the other ends of 4 of these to 4 of the coins.

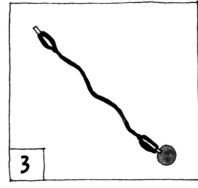

3 Clip the sixth remaining lead to the last copper coin.

Oozing Batteries!

The chemicals inside batteries are not nice. They have names like cadmium, manganese dioxide, ammonium chloride, and lithium thionyl chloride. They are definitely not good for you. Sometimes batteries will leak inside your electronic equipment. If you can see that something has oozed out of a battery, you must dispose of it carefully and then give your hands a really good wash.

The chemicals in batteries can harm the environment when they are just chucked away in our trash. You could try to find out if your town has a special place where batteries can be disposed of more safely.

4 Line up the beakers. Place the foil squares and coins inside them as shown.

Make sure none of the foil squares and coins are touching inside the mugs.

5 Place the coin which is on its own on a lead in one of the end beakers.

6 Place the foil which is on its own on a lead in the other end beaker.

foil

coin

7 Connect the free end of the lead attached to the coin to the long leg (+) of the LED.

8 Connect the free end of the lead attached to the foil to the short leg (-) of the LED.

Turn off the lights—you can see the LED glow!

Try This!

To make your battery really strong, see if you can get the foil and coins as close as possible without touching each other.

The Electrons

Your Briny Battery is creating a chemical reaction that releases electrons. Each cup of saltwater containing a coin and foil gives the electrons more energy. It's as if each cup is a rung on a ladder, and the LED is the diving board. When you have enough rungs, the electrons can reach the diving board and jump off, making their splashes of light as they do so.

135

Mighty Magnet

Did you know that where you've got electricity, you've got magnetism too? When electrons move around they make a magnetic force. You can use this force to turn an iron rod, like a screwdriver, into a magnet. You need to coil some wire around the metal and connect it up to a battery. The more wire you coil around the rod, the stronger your electromagnet will be.

Your screwdriver may still pick up light objects, like paper clips, even when the electric current is switched off. This is because it is possible to make the screwdriver permanently magnetic!

What you will need:
- 1x 9-volt PP3 battery
- 2 crocodile clip leads
- 13 feet insulated wire
- 1 medium screwdriver with a plastic handle
- scissors
- clear tape
- paper clip

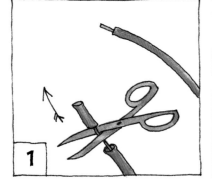

1 Use the scissors to strip a small bit of plastic from both ends of the wire.

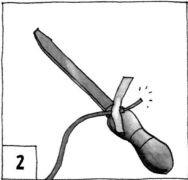

2 Tape one end of the wire to the handle of the screwdriver. Leave the stripped wire clear of tape.

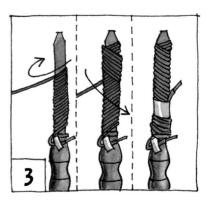

3 Wrap the wire as neatly as you can around the shaft of the screwdriver to make a coil. Go back over the first coil to make a second one. Tape the wire to hold it in place.

Scrapyard Magnets

Powerful electromagnets are used in many industries to lift and move really heavy metal objects. In junkyards they can be attached to cranes to lift scrap metal like old, bashed-up cars.

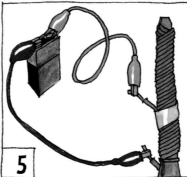

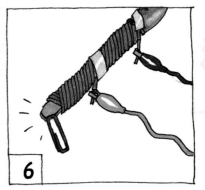

Clip one end of a lead to one end of the coil. Clip the other end of this lead to the positive (+) side of the battery.

Clip one end of the other lead to the remaining free end of the coil. Clip the other end of this lead to the negative (-) side of the battery.

Try picking up the paper clip with the screwdriver. Remove a crocodile clip from the battery to switch the magnet off.

WARNING!
Be careful, as the battery may get a bit warm! It's best to disconnect the battery after a short while.

The Electrons

When an electron moves, you get a little magnetic field. If all the electrons move together, like through the coil of wire, you get a very strong magnetic field that can be used to pick things up. In the coil, the electrons are all whizzing around, just like a corkscrew on a rollercoaster ride! If you keep the electric coil on for long enough, the electrons in the screwdriver also start to move in a synchronized way. It's as if they have been taught to line dance by all the electrons in the coil!

Cool Compass

You can make your own compass by magnetizing a needle. The sort of magnet you need for this is a bar magnet with a N and S marked on it to show you which is the North Pole and the South Pole of the magnet. When you compare your results with a real compass you will be amazed!

What you will need:
- 1 needle
- 1 bar magnet
- small piece of paper towel
- 1 plastic cup or beaker
- compass (for checking purposes only!)

1

Fill the cup or beaker with water. Take the needle between your thumb and forefinger.

2

Hold the magnet in your other hand with the North end touching the eye of the needle.

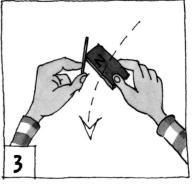

3

Stroke the North end of the magnet down the needle starting at the eye end. Do this several times from the eye to the point.

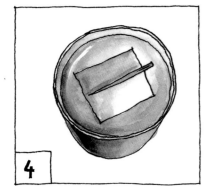

4

Float the piece of paper towel on the surface of the water. Gently place the needle on it.

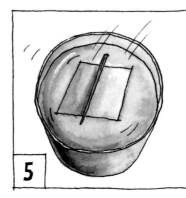

5

Watch the needle and paper towel turn on the water. The eye of the needle will point North!

Get your real compass and you will be able to check this is true!

Mega Lava

Inside the earth is an enormous mass of swirling, molten rocks and metals. These rocks and metals flow in a particular shape and they create an electric current. This amazing electric current also makes a magnetic field in a particular shape. Using incredibly powerful computers, scientists have been able to recreate the shape of this magnetic field. We call the top of this shape the North Pole and the bottom the South Pole, and a compass tells you which way is North and which is South.

Magnets also have a North pole and a South pole. The south end of a magnet will be attracted to the north end of another magnet—and so the south end of our magnetized needle is attracted to the North Pole of the Earth!

Mythical Magnets

There is a story about an Ancient Greek shepherd boy called Magnes. He was out and about tending his flocks when the iron tip of his crook and the iron nails in his sandals got stuck to the ground! He had found stones containing a naturally magnetic mineral which we now call magnetite. But it's really named after an area called Magnesia, now in modern Turkey, where loads of these rocks can be found.

Crazy Currents

We can make a nifty gadget to show there is an electric current flowing through a wire. If we put a compass inside a coil of wire attached to a battery, the compass will move. This is because of the magnetic field created by the electric current in the wire.

What you will need:
- 1x 9-volt PP3 battery
- 2 crocodile clip leads
- 13 feet of insulated wire
- scissors
- 1 small compass
- plastic top from an aerosol can
- clear tape
- sticky tack or Plasticine

1 Use the scissors to strip a little bit of plastic from both ends of the wire.

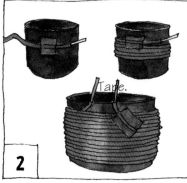

2 Tape one end of the wire to the can top. Wind the wire around the can top. Make a second coil on top of the first.

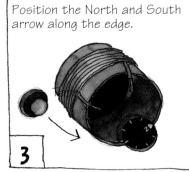

Position the North and South arrow along the edge.

3 Put a blob of sticky tack or Plasticine on the back of the compass. Push it down on the edge of the can top.

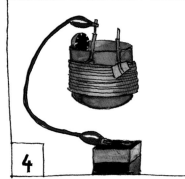

4 Clip one end of a lead to one end of the wire coil. Clip the other end of this lead to the positive (+) side of the battery.

5 Clip one end of the other lead to the remaining free end of the coil. Clip the other end to the negative (-) side of the battery.

6 The compass needle will swing in one direction, showing you that there is a current passing through the wire.

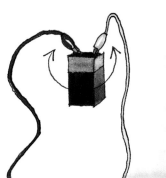

Try This!

Now swap the clips around so that you change the terminals they are clipped to. Watch the compass needle swing in the opposite direction.

Father of the Amp

You'll have seen the word "amp" on electrical bits and pieces. Amps are named after a man called André Marie Ampère (1775-1836) who was handy with his circuits. Electrical currents are measured in amps in the same way as the length of something can be measured in inches. An ammeter is the name of the gadget that measures them. Electronic ammeters are used in lots of portable equipment, like laptops and cameras, to work out how much longer the battery will last.

The Electrons

What are they up to now? The electrons are whizzing around the coil of wire as if they are on a rollercoaster. When you change the clips round on the terminals of the batteries they all change direction and zoom round the rollercoaster backwards! This then makes the magnetic field go in the opposite direction, and the compass flicks the other way.

Break Dancing Magnet

In Crazy Currents we turned electricity into movement to show that there was an electric current. Electricity can also be changed into movement to make a noise. We can do a wacky thing with a magnet on some thread to show this movement. Use the can top with the wire around it from the previous experiment (remove the compass first!)

To make a sound that our ears can hear, the movement has to be very fast and it has to move a lot of air. In a loudspeaker there is a moving coil connected to a cone-shaped piece of paper, which helps the loudspeaker move the right amount of air so that our ears can hear a noise—or music!

What you will need:
- 1x 9-volt PP3 battery
- 2 crocodile clip leads
- can top with wire coiled around it from page 140
- 1 small round magnet
- scissors
- sticky tack
- cotton thread

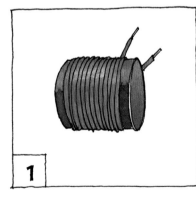

1

Lie the can top on its side.

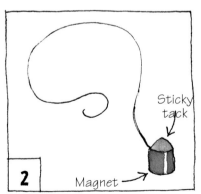

2

Stick the magnet on the end of a length of thread using a blob of sticky tack.

Sticky tack

Magnet

3

Clip one end of a lead to the positive (+) side of the battery. Clip the other end to one end of the wire coil.

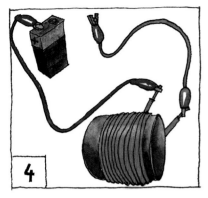

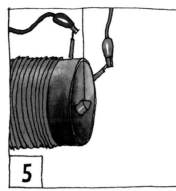

Clip one end of the other lead to the other end of the wire coil.

Dangle the magnet on the thread in front of the open end of the can top.

Touch the negative (-) side of the battery with the unattached crocodile clip.

Watch that magnet dance!

Waves of Sound

A microphone works in the opposite way to a loudspeaker. It turns small movement from the sound waves of someone speaking or singing into an electric current. This current is so small that it is difficult to do an experiment to show how it works without doing more tricky electronics.

Cool Conclusions

So what have we found out?

- Electrons whiz around wire in electric circuits.
- You can use electrons to make light in a lightbulb and an LED.
- You can use electrons to make magnets.
- You can control the electrons with resistors.
- You can make electric circuits using water and salt as well as wires.
- You can change electric current into movement using magnetic fields.
- There is swirling molten lava inside the earth that produces magnetic fields.
- Light and radio waves are special waves of electricity and magnetism that travel very fast.

Scientists and engineers have turned all of these weird things into useful gadgets and gizmos that we use in everyday life—everything from computers to flashlights. And they are still inventing more! Would you like to invent something?

Electronspeak

Amp = how many electrons are flowing.
Volt = how much energy the electrons have.
Resistance = how difficult it is for the electrons to move around.
Magnetism = what you get when electrons move.
Electromagnetic wave = wriggly mix of electricity and magnetism that moves very fast. Includes light waves and radio waves but radio waves are not as wriggly as light waves!